CREATIVE
MACHINE KNITTING

CREATIVE
MACHINE KNITTING

SALLY-ANNE ELLIOTT

Fashion photography by Ursula Steiger

BARRON'S

New York • Toronto

Creative Machine Knitting
First U.S. edition published 1989 by Barron's Educational Series.
Text and illustrations © 1989 Frances Lincoln Limited.

Creative Machine Knitting was conceived, edited and produced by
Frances Lincoln Limited, Apollo Works, 5 Charlton Kings Road, London NW5 2SB.

International Standard Book Number: 0-8120-5940-9
Library of Congress Catalog Card No. 88-8127

Library of Congress Cataloging-in-Publication Data

Elliott, Sally-Anne.
Creative machine knitting.

Includes index.
1. Knitting, Machine. I. Title.
TT680.E45   1989   746.9'2
ISBN 0-8120-5940-9

Typeset in Linotron 10/12 Garamond Light ITC
by Bookworm Typesetting, Manchester
Printed and bound in Hong Kong

246897531

All inquiries should be addressed to:
Barron's Educational Series, Inc.
250 Wireless Boulevard
Hauppauge, New York 11788

CONTENTS

FOREWORD

Within this book I hope to inspire machine knitters to produce classic, well-finished, wearable garments. I also hope the book will encourage knitters to create their own fabrics and use them in garments they design themselves.

The collection of garments is treated very much as I would design a commercial collection for a company. It is divided into four groups that cover clothing for all occasions, yet which still hang together as a collection. Attention to detail is emphasized throughout and I hope that this will encourage you to look at your own creations as critically as you might view those on sale in shops.

Although I designed the garments to be made as they are shown, I hope that the section on stitches and fabrics will encourage you to use the basic shapes in conjunction with your own fabric and design ideas. I really want to motivate knitters to spend more time developing fabrics, sampling and working through all aspects of a design before starting to knit. My fashion drawings will suggest to you how to explore the use of alternative fabrics for the garments, and in the following eight pages I have shown how you could start working from source, gradually translating a design through to a shape and making decisions about finish and detail.

The measurement diagrams given with each garment pattern also show shaping instructions. Try using them for quick reference; eventually you will be able to make your own diagrams and work straight from them. If you have a charting device use the diagrams to translate the shape.

So that this book can be used with any type of standard gauge machine, I have included a section at the end of the book which will enable you to match up the functions on your machine to the abbreviations used in my pattern writing. I find single bed domestic machines very useful for most of my work, but owners of all types and brands of machine, including Passap, will be able to follow my instructions. The punchcards are supplied in 24- and 40-stitch repeats, and instructions are given for adapting them for machines that have a 60-stitch repeat.

I have included a section on double bed techniques which concentrates on extending the possibilities of fabric development and finishing techniques on these machines. This will be of interest to those who want to use them for more than producing simple ribs.

In the chapter on technical information I have shown many of my preferred methods, some of which you may be familiar with, others you may not have seen before. I find them all extremely useful, and I feel that in many cases they will give you more useful technical insight into the capabilities of your machine than many of the machine manuals.

One of the aspects of machine knitting that I am keen to emphasize very strongly is working by hand on the machine to produce structures that cannot be obtained automatically, by using hand transfer and hand tooling for instance. In all the patterns for both fabrics and garments, provision has been made for knitters with all the gadgets, and knitters with none. Those who are inclined towards more complex, time-consuming work are encouraged to produce garments such as the gansey suit (page 102). Undoubtedly this piece takes a lot of knitting time, but the design options open to the knitter when working in this way are limitless. Knitters who wish to make pieces more quickly with less detail could work the suit with none of the hand tooling and it would still make a beautiful outfit.

The whole point of this book is to inspire a new approach, and to motivate knitters to work beyond the boundaries they may encounter when knitting on a machine.

Author's Acknowledgments

I would like to thank Frances Lincoln for enabling me to do this book and Susan Berry for her help in the early stages. I would also like to thank Charyn Jones who has helped enormously with the writing and has put a vast amount into many other aspects of this book. I am very grateful to Louise Tucker for her work on the design of this book and also Susanne Haines for helping to put the book together.

I must say a special thank you to Ursula Steiger for the fashion photography, and Moritz for assisting. Also thank you to Barbara Jones for make-up, and to Eleanor, Annie, Amelia, Liz, Lou Lou and Jane for modeling. Thank you to Mr. Paul Smith for lending clothes and accessories.

I am very grateful to Stephen Sheard and Kathleen Hargreaves of Rowan Yarns for all their assistance and for supplying yarn. I would also like to thank Todd & Duncan for supplying cashmere yarn for the dressy sweater.

I would like to thank my knitters, Pat Jones, Lillian Payne, Sandra Lennox, Carol Barnard and Tula Petito; also Mrs. Coombes for her help with washing and shrinking. I am eternally grateful to Monica Bywaters for all her help and support in all aspects of this book. I must also thank Ralph Compton and Sophie Fielding for all their support. A special thank you to Mr. Derek Morten for helping with everything.

Finally I would like to thank my mother, Barbara Elliott, for her support and encouragement with my work.

Sally-Anne Elliott

INTRODUCTION

ELEMENTS OF DESIGN

The most important part of any knitwear design is the fabric; even with good shape, styling and finish, your design will be truly successful only if the fabric has the perfect combination of texture, color and pattern. Fabric construction and development need plenty of preparation and thought as well as sampling on the machine to work through all the possibilities of the machine and the yarns.

You can start either with the fabric or the shape; you may already know what you want to design, or perhaps you have an existing fabric that you would like to see knitted into a garment. Obviously many of your ideas will come from garments or styles that you have seen and liked. If you have definite ideas, you may want to turn now to the pattern making section (page 18).

Knitwear design starts with an initial idea – texture, shape, or even an interesting photograph or exhibition. Inspiration can be gained from the most unusual sources and you should not limit yourself to the obvious, such as textiles, books and paintings, but leave yourself open to any influences. That way you have a good opportunity of creating something that is fresh both visually and technically.

IDEAS

Basically anything that you find exciting can be your starting point as long as you keep an open mind about the way you manipulate the materials and techniques to create the effect you require. An interesting way to start is by choosing from more than one source – for example, I have collected items for the collage opposite from Nature, and manufactured items such as pottery and wallpapers. These combinations may sound rather unusual, but by taking the color from one element, and the patterning from another, you will find that you can be led to conclusions that you would never have reached otherwise.

Putting ideas onto paper can be a daunting task but there are several ways you can overcome any apprehension. A sketchbook is whatever you want to make it. To get ideas onto paper start by collecting things which relate to your sources – bits of fabric, yarn, postcards, colored paper, net, beads, shells and clippings from magazines. Photocopy relevant things together; you will be surprised at the interesting effects you get, especially if you try reducing or enlarging on the machine. Using scissors and paste start to build up a collage of color, texture and shape. You can add finer details with a pencil or colored crayons and as you gain more confidence, make marks with paint or pastel and mix different media together, then add collage on top.

It is important to relax and work in the way that suits

you – free, detailed or a mixture of both. Gradually, as you become more confident, you will be able to control the media to produce the images you want. If you are aiming at something that you think is beyond your artistic capabilities, find a photograph, photocopy it and work on the photocopy. Color photocopying is still quite expensive but it is an exciting medium to work with; anyone with access to such a machine should make full use of it. You can buy stitch-related graph paper or tracing paper, which allows for the shape of the stitch (page 135), or you can work straight over a photograph or image.

When you feel that you have done enough research, start choosing suitable yarns and colors and think about which machine-knitting technique is most suitable for your design. Collect shade cards and bits of yarn to work with in conjunction with your sketchbook.

SAMPLING

To decide which techniques and yarns could be suitable for your design, you need to make a sample. Sampling is absolutely essential if you want to create something new and original that works. You won't be wasting time or yarn because you will find out what a really good combination of yarn and pattern is by your mistakes or successes. Every sample should be labeled and kept; they all come in useful.

Start with a specific stitch or pattern and work through the yarn you have on hand. Alter the gauge; look at the work from the reverse-side – it may be a more interesting fabric; introduce different colorways. You don't need to bind off at every change; you can knit a few rows in waste yarn between samples. Look at the way the different yarns or textures alter the face of the fabric. The same stitch in different colors may look different. Feel the fabric. If it is at the right gauge it should look and feel right; not too loose or too tight.

The next step is to mix techniques. Refer to pages 22–63 for stitch and fabric ideas. If you need to make a punchcard, graph it out and try it, then make any necessary adjustments. Holes punched in error can be filled in with sticky labels or tape. Sort out the exact specifications of your fabric, such as yarn type and gauge setting, and record them.

When sampling, you must look carefully at each sample and learn from it so that the next one is slightly improved until you have exactly what you want. There is no need to waste time and yarn sampling enormous swatches at this stage. They need only be big enough to get a clear view so that you can make adjustments. The swatch should be big enough to show your whole pattern and any repeats horizontally and vertically, to give the overall impression.

Sampling is the most time-consuming part of knitwear design and you will find that the extra effort spent getting things right at the beginning will produce a superior result and save time when knitting and making-up problems have to be solved.

COLOR

Choosing colors is not just a matter of personal taste, or what is fashionable this year. Color selection is a technical problem as well. You may decide on a single color motif on a plain background, or mixing colors up in a Fair Isle or jacquard; color can be isolated to emphasize a stitch or texture. Colors can create different illusions; dark colors tend to be slenderizing and light colors the opposite, so use this to your advantage when mixing colors within one outfit.

When you choose colors you should do so in a natural light; artificial light distorts the true shades. It is also important to see an adequate amount of the yarn. Tiny fringes, like paint charts, can be deceptive. It is best to put several balls, or cones, or knitted pieces of fabric together to see the color in a larger area. Try to look at the colors of yarns in the correct ratio. For example, if you want a navy sweater with tiny touches of very bright colors, look at a large area of navy with small pieces of the brights; that way you will get a true idea of the image you are creating.

To help with your color sketchbook, cut up paper, photographs, small swatch books (available from art shops) and use felt-tip pens. Yarn spinners provide extensive shade cards. Use these in conjunction with your paper work to see how the color looks as a fiber rather than on paper. I use an old sewing thread chart for color, but paint charts and wallpaper books would also be useful.

A camera is a useful tool for collecting color and source material. I find it is a great help to look through my photograph collection for ideas. Alternatively, photograph specific things such as walls, flowers, animals. Natural sources are inspirational; colors not normally used together often work well in nature. Look closely and you'll get good and worthwhile results.

Computers now play a large part in textile design and are invaluable for working out colorways and putting designs into repeat, printing out graphs and written patterns. Software for monochrome work can be purchased relatively cheaply; color work is more expensive to set up but obviously has endless possibilities. If you have access to a computer, get someone to explain the program to you.

MIXING COLORS

When you start to work colors together, you will notice how they react against each other and you can learn to make adjustments as you sample. For example, if you put yellow next to red they will read as orange where they meet. This can be developed further by running two ends through the same feeder to produce a marbled look. It is just like mixing paints and the rules are the same – blue and yellow will look green. Close combinations will give a glowing effect. To merge colors further, you can twist the two ends together so they fade into each other. You can see from the swatches and drawings opposite how color combinations can be built up from your sketchbook.

Some manufacturers have ends of yarns spun together in different colors to give the illusion that there are more than two colors in one row. This tends to soften Fair Isle, for example. Working in this way you can make rich multi-color fabrics. Sewing cotton is effective for this technique because it is shiny.

TEXTURE

Creating texture in machine knitting is easy. There are so many different stitch effects and it is possible to control and combine them to form exciting structures. (Structure is a technical word used in knitting. It relates to the make-up of the stitch.) For example, hand texture (page 32) is versatile and you can mix it with almost anything, whereas tucking (page 30) can be limiting and requires planning, though it is far quicker to produce. Other obvious texture techniques are slip stitch, cables and weaving or using odd materials (pages 38, 40, 42, 56) or textural yarns. Generally speaking you can do far more with texture than the manufacturers' manuals lead you to believe. It is just a matter of experimenting.

Traditional handknit designs provide endless examples of good use of texture which can easily be adapted for use in machine knitting. For instance, fishermen's sweaters display a good use of cables, purl and moss stitches.

YARNS

There are many types of yarn available to the machine knitter and it is always best to try out the yarn first by sampling. Obviously this is not always possible, especially if you are dealing with companies by mail, which you must do if you are to have access to a large selection of materials at lower prices.

When you make your choice you must determine:
o The type of the yarn – marl, slub, loop, tape – in other words, the structure or construction of the yarn.
o The composition – cotton, wool, silk, or mixed percentages – that is the fiber or material the yarn is made from.
The color (if you are not dyeing your own). If you decide to use a different color from the one you have sampled, you will find that the gauge could be changed because certain dyes affect the yarn.
o Thickness – often referred to as the "count" in industry. There are many different systems and I don't think it necessary for you to understand them. You can make a different thickness by using several strands of yarn together to increase the ply. An extra strand is called an end. Handknitting yarns are usually too thick for machine knitting and they are usually sold in small balls.

BUYING FROM SHOPS

This is a simple, though rather expensive way to acquire your materials; you have the advantage of seeing and feeling the merchandise. Look for a commercial pattern which resembles the garment you want to make and note the type and thickness of yarn. If you are not sure, buy the smallest amount to make a sample to test gauge and texture. Specialist wool shops will sometimes wind off a small amount for sampling purposes, so ask before you purchase large amounts if you are not sure. It is a good idea to make small samples from yarn you have at home before going to the shop so that you can get a better idea of what you are looking for. Better still, show the assistant who will then be able to point out similar materials in stock or perhaps refer you to another supplier.

BUYING BY MAIL

Call or send for yarn manufacturers' shade cards. Once you have dealt with a company, efficient suppliers will automatically send you up-dates of types and colors as their ranges develop. Select your colors from the suppliers' cards. It will soon become obvious which supplier is best for you. It is a good idea to combine orders with friends so that you can obtain yarn at a competitive or wholesale price.

When you receive yarn, remove the label from the inside of the cone and stick it into a book together with a wrapping, or length, of the relevant yarn. This will serve as an invaluable reference book when dealing with commercial suppliers.

GETTING YARNS TO KNIT

Some yarns may prove difficult to sample and there are several ways in which you can get around this. You can feed in by hand. You might need to wax or spray the yarn to help it run through the machine smoothly; use a device specially made to wax yarn (page 140); or a commercial spray.

The equivalent of a knitting worsted thickness is probably the thickest you would want for trouble-free knitting on a standard gauge machine. I have seen students force all manner of things through reluctant machinery with most interesting results, however. If you are interested in experimenting in this way, I suggest you keep an old machine for this purpose. If your design requires small touches of a hefty chenille or bouclé, you could knit manually in small areas or work on every other needle and isolate the area using the holding or intarsia technique. This gives almost as much control as with handknitting and cuts down the risk of damage to the machinery, while opening up the yarn choice.

TWISTING

Many interesting yarns can be made by twisting two or more together and knitting machine manufacturers now produce twisters for domestic use. Fine mercerized cotton (sewing thread is good, though buy in bulk as it is expensive) can produce wonderful speckled effects when twisted with other yarns.

Textured yarns can also be mixed, but you need to find very fine yarns to twist together to get a good effect and produce a workable yarn.

The only drawback when using a hand-wound twister is that you are limited to the length of yarn you can twist at one time by the size of the spool, which is too small for a complete garment. There are other types of twister which stand on cones at different levels and combine the yarns as you knit (page 140). Alternatively, some spinning companies will twist yarns to your specifications.

DYEING

Dyeing yarn is a rewarding and worthwhile task for the avid knitter. It can be easy too, with domestic dyes which can be used in washing machines.
o You must always dye on hank and keep the fibers straight. A good tip is to draw them out of the water so that the weight of the water pulls the fibers down, thus straightening them.
o The hanks must be loosely secured with small ties which will also help keep the yarn tidy. Experiment and

you will see how easy it is.

"Space" dyeing uses several colors – four is the most common. A quarter of the hank is dipped into each color so that when you wind off the yarn, it is multi-colored. It knits up differently on different widths of fabric; narrow pieces have a more blocked effect with the colors merging into each other and larger expanses look much more random.

Spotting is as its name suggests. To make spotted yarn just mix up several different colors of dye and paint spots onto the hank.

Natural dyeing is not complicated and you will be surprised at the range of colors when you work with berries, mosses etc. It is possible to produce shades that you will never see in the shops.

UNCONVENTIONAL YARNS

Materials other than yarns are especially manufactured for machine knitting and they can be used within machine-made fabrics and garments.

It is a good idea to invest in an old or second-hand machine (which can be picked up very cheaply) and keep it for work of this type so that you can experiment fully without fear of damaging your best machine. However, many of the ideas included on page 56 will not harm your machine at all so please read on even if you cannot find a second machine.

A good guideline to follow when working with unconventional materials is to do everything possible to get the machine to work. For example, if you have a number of lengths rather than one continuous yarn, you must hold it and hand feed it into the carriage. This is useful when working with difficult or badly wound yarns,

or many different cones or types of yarn at one time; rethreading can be laborious.

Most of the odd materials I use can be knitted through the normal threading process (the antenna or mast) of the machine. You will find that you have to change gauge more often during knitting, especially if you are using different thicknesses together.

You can knit with almost anything that vaguely resembles yarn as long as it is strong enough not to snap, and soft enough not to damage your needles – string, braid, raffia, soft wire, wire covering, plastic strips, twisted paper, polythene strips, fabric, leather, etc.

Collect odd balls or cones of string. Shiny plastic-type string can be found quite easily and sometimes in several colors. The advantage colorwise of working with unusual materials is that it is easier to apply color to them. String, raffia and paper can be colored with felt-tip pens. If you cut strips thin enough, you can seal tape, colored paper or anything else between two strips of adhesive tape to make a colored plastic yarn.

ESTIMATING YARN AMOUNTS

This is not easy. You can weigh your sample and estimate the square area of your finished garment from the measurement diagram and divide by the sample size. Then multiply the number of times your sample goes into the garment shape by the weight of the sample. More accurately, you can knit up a ball of your chosen yarn, then calculate the area one ball knits up and divide that into the area of the finished design to determine the number of balls.

A rough guide to work from is that a sleeve or back of a sweater is roughly one quarter of the total yarn.

STYLING & SHAPE

To translate your fabric and shape ideas into a garment, you also need to make decisions about trims, finishes and joining methods, and when you have all the specifications, you can make the pattern. Making patterns for knitted garments is really quite simple.

If you have already decided what sort of fabric you would like to use, you should work from a sample knitted to the correct gauge in the correct yarn. You must have the exact gauge before you write the final pattern and if a collar, for example, is required, it must be sampled too.

DRAWING THE SHAPE

The two-stage process before you make the pattern involves a drawing to help you visualize the finished garment, and a diagram with the exact measurements to knit to. These two stages sometimes overlap.

You may have collected pictures from magazines or seen a design somewhere that you want to reproduce. For most people, the main problem when you first begin to design is visualizing these ideas. This can be easily overcome by tracing figures from magazines or working over photocopies. A template is provided for you to trace off and use which can be adapted to the shape you require (page 19). When you do this fashion drawing, put in details such as collars and finishes.

All details for edgings, collars and finishes must be decided now so that the information is on hand before you make the pattern. Be careful with garments in multi-color fabrics; the trims must be matched unless they are designed to contrast, otherwise they will cause an outline effect.

When you are designing it is important to keep the garment simple. Knitting stretches and it is easy to over-design and give yourself problems. You have to be careful to avoid too many seams as they tend to look unsightly. They work best when they perform a specific function, such as for shaping or yokes. Watch out when designing garments made from pieces which are too wide for the machine. Although most machines have 200 needles, some fabrics relax to a narrower width. The same applies to fibers such as lambswool which can shrink considerably after pressing or finishing.

To begin with, it is a good idea to stick to shapes and necklines that you know will suit you, and then experiment further when you are more confident with pattern writing and knitting. Make sure you choose lines that are flattering to your figure. Avoid raglan sleeves if you don't want to accentuate your shoulders, for example, and add shoulder pads for more structure.

Familiarize yourself with the seaming details I have used in this book to add decorative finishing touches in the collection. On the T-shirt alternative (see opposite), eyelets were worked along the seams. I also worked a tiny eyelet detail along the edges of the ribbed inset. Often it is possible to overcome technical problems and enhance the design at the same time. For example, on the slacks the pieces are bound off together which not only looks good, but also forms a chain that helps to keep the shape in the leg and at the seat (see bottom left).

COMPLETING THE DESIGN

Working through a design is a logical process. It is a combination of styling, fabric development, sizing and detail specifications that goes into forming a garment that works. It is important to remember to put in and take out what is necessary to make your design work rather than taking ideas too literally. For example, in the shirt on page 72 I used a shirt collar, but lowered the neckline, and the sleeve is hardly shaped.

The trims look straightforward, but in fact at the first sampling stage they looked heavy, so I decided to work them much tighter at the turning point, then at least two numbers tighter on the welt section. This also prevented them from flaring out as welts often do. The tight rows to turn the edge would have worked had they been loose rows, but I wanted a sharp edge.

I wanted to use seam detail in this garment. It is so plain I could afford to and it shows up nicely. This means that it has to be done well because the mistakes will also show. Because of the simplicity of this shirt, I introduced wale deflection wherever I could fit it in. It worked naturally on the shaped sections but the straight side seams took a little more thought. I think it is essential to consider all aspects of the garment, even under the arms.

The collar was a bit tricky because the single bed fabric curls so much. This was easily remedied by adding a tiny binding which curls the other way.

Once the welt problem was solved, the placket was easy to organize and I added a bit more chain detail by binding off on the right side as on the seams; it was just a matter of matching things up. The detail in the center front looks simple and subtle but I started off transferring every row. This caused terrible distortion, so I changed it to every fourth row, which looked fine.

It really is a case of choosing some guidelines and working within them so that your garment hangs together technically and visually. The most difficult part of designing is getting what you have visualized to work technically. For example, in order to get the shirt front wale deflection detail as I wanted, I had to have a small plain section before the placket starts because I could not work in the normal way (transferring the stitches outwards from the center) until there was an opening to work from.

PATTERN MAKING

Before making the pattern, you must draw the measurement diagram. Use a good-quality dressmaker's tape. Look in the mirror or use existing garments to determine lengths, yoke depths and pocket positions. For chest and hip fit and sizing you will want to include ease in your finished measurements. The garments in the collection have very generous amounts for ease. The chart below may help you decide which effect you want and therefore which measurements to use on your diagram for the chest and for the length of the front and back. Remember when calculating the sleeve length to allow for a dropped shoulder. Armhole drop varies from 22cm (8½in) for a fitted armhole to 25cm (10in) for a loose fit. For a garment under which other clothes are to be worn, a further amount of ease should be allowed.

Actual chest measurement	standard	loose	very roomy
	Finished measurements for chest		
81cm/32in	86cm/34in	91cm/36in	94cm/37in
86cm/34in	91cm/36in	96cm/38in	99cm/39in
91cm/36in	96cm/38in	101cm/40in	104cm/41in
96cm/38in	101cm/40in	106cm/42in	109cm/43in
101cm/40in	106cm/42in	112cm/44in	114cm/45in
	Finished measurements for length from shoulder to hip		
81cm/32in	53cm/21in	55cm/22in	57cm/22½in
86cm/34in	57cm/22½in	60cm/24in	65cm/25½in
91cm/36in	58cm/23in	61cm/24¼in	68cm/26½in
96cm/38in	59cm/23¼in	62cm/24½in	70cm/27½in
101cm/40in	60cm/24in	63cm/25in	70cm/27½in

To make your pattern, you will need the following:
○ Your personal measurements, including ease.
○ A drawing of your garment with its measurements, details of finishes and trims clearly marked so that it is easy to work from. Allow for welts, length of rib, armholes, depth of neck and position of pockets.
○ A relaxed sample of the structure you wish to use in the correct yarn knitted to the correct gauge – 15.5cm (6in) square minimum.
○ Samples of trims in the correct yarn knitted on the correct gauge.
○ A tape or ruler for measurements and stitch counting.
○ A calculator – optional, but time-saving.

The next step is to measure your gauge. It is important that the sample is allowed to relax (for at least four hours) before measuring. Lightly steam or press the sample and lay it on a flat surface.

Now count the number of stitches to 2.5cm (1in). Notice the prominent lines down the fabric; these are the wales. When you have the stitch count, then count the rows to 2.5cm (1in). Write this information onto your diagram, and then count the stitches and rows to 10cm (4in). Record this information in the same way. Make both measurements to check that there is no difference.

The next step is to transfer the information about the shape of the garment from centimeters or inches into rows (R) and stitches (sts). Stitches go across the machine and rows go up and down the machine. If you have a gauge of 8 sts = 2.5cm (1in) and 32 sts = 10cm (4in), and 11 R = 2.5cm (1in) and 44 R = 10cm (4in), and the garment is 60cm (24in) long, then you simply multiply 4.4R by 60cm or 11 R by 24in = 264. If you have an odd number for the length and the 2.5cm (1in) count did show a difference from the 10cm (4in) count, add the odd centimeter or inch according to your calculations on a 2.5cm (1in) count. This may seem a bit complicated, but it will become clearer when you do it.

Work through your diagram and convert all the measurements into stitches or rows, breaking down curves, such as necklines, into horizontal, vertical and diagonal lines. Diagonal lines are worked as follows. Take the measurements at the top and bottom, and convert to stitches. For example, let us say that the bottom measurement is 50cm (20in), and the top 55cm (22in). Subtract the top from the bottom to give the difference in centimeters, in this case 5cm (2in). If 8 sts = 2.5cm (1in), then 5cm (2in) will be 16 stitches in total. You need to divide this figure in two for each side of the garment. This leaves 8. So you need to increase a total of 8 stitches each side over the number of rows knitted.

In this example there will be 264 rows. Divide this number by the number of stitches to increase. 264 ÷ 8 = 33. So you would increase 1 stitch each side every 33 rows, 8 times. This will balance the increases nicely throughout the garment part.

Sleeves are shaped as diagonal lines, but at both edges. Split necklines into sections, and if you have a difficult line to knit, put it onto graph paper counting 1 square as 1 stitch and 1 row. Stitch-related graph paper is the best.

You can knit straight from your diagram, or use a charting device (page 140) if you have one with your machine and if you prefer to work that way. If you have a repeat, you will need to work out your placing and you may need to add a few extra stitches onto the width or length of the garment to accommodate the design.

Some people find it easy to work from diagrams, but if you want to write out your pattern, you simply start at the bottom of the diagram and write "cast on x sts and work straight for y R". However, remember that it is not possible to measure knitting accurately while it is still on the machine.

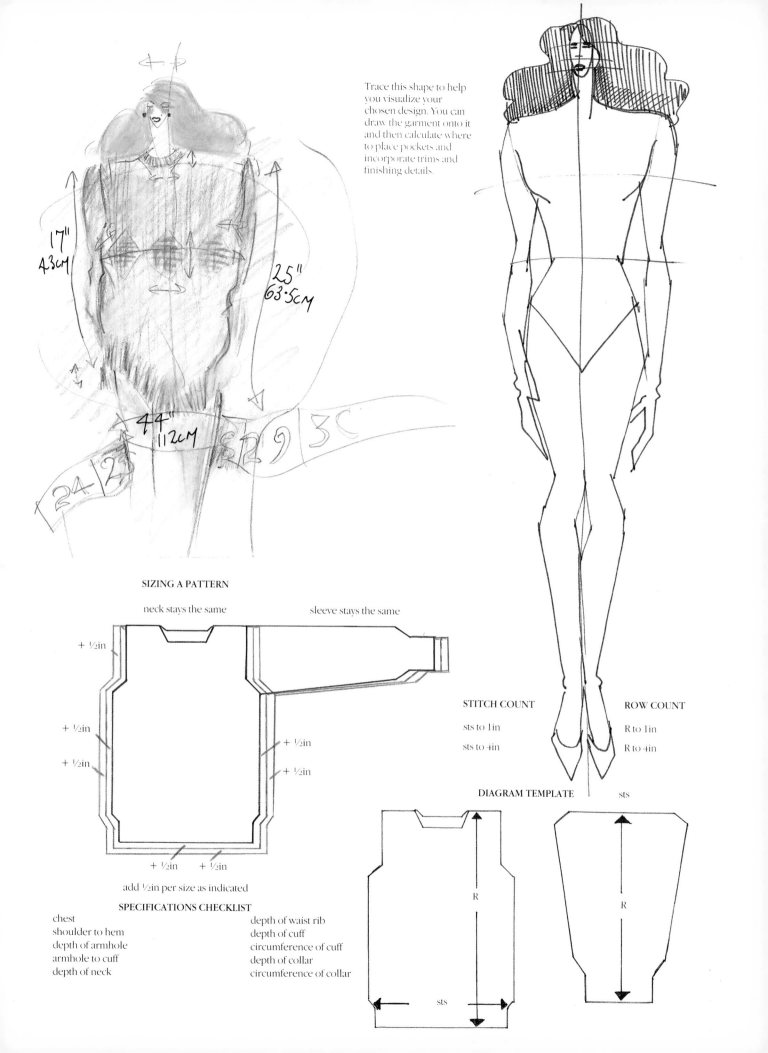

17"
43CM

25"
63·5CM

44"
112CM

24 2 8 2 9 3C

Trace this shape to help
you visualize your
chosen design. You can
draw the garment onto it
and then calculate where
to place pockets and
incorporate trims and
finishing details.

SIZING A PATTERN

neck stays the same   sleeve stays the same

+ ½in

+ ½in

+ ½in

+ ½in

+ ½in

+ ½in   + ½in

add ½in per size as indicated

STITCH COUNT

sts to 1in

sts to 4in

ROW COUNT

R to 1in

R to 4in

DIAGRAM TEMPLATE   sts

SPECIFICATIONS CHECKLIST

chest   depth of waist rib
shoulder to hem   depth of cuff
depth of armhole   circumference of cuff
armhole to cuff   depth of collar
depth of neck   circumference of collar

R

R

sts

STITCHES & FABRICS

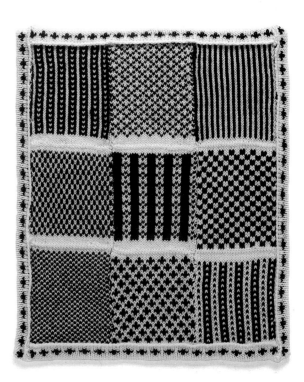

STRIPES

When you are designing a striped garment, you must take care to use the color and stripes so that they are flattering. It is also important to consider the technical difficulties, such as yarns being "left" at the wrong side of the machine. You need to take care when mixing different qualities of yarn. If the yarns are very different counts, this can distort the edges. You can solve this problem by altering gauges, although this can lead to longer knitting time so anticipate any problems of this type during the sampling stages.

Beginners often tend to work only with stripes that are divisible by two so that all the yarns are left at the same end of the machine and loose ends are avoided, but with a little forethought you can have stripes made up of odd numbers of rows.

The one-row stripe (2) was worked using the free move (FM) or non-knit facility, taking the carriage back empty on FM to pick up the colors at whichever end they finished. This method is particularly useful for odd row stripes,

multi-color stripes, or various depths of stripe.

When working on deep stripes, watch the loops at the edges. If you must jump a large number of rows with a color, either break off the yarn and sew in the ends, or weave the ends in as you go. Do not carry too many yarns up the seams or it will spoil the hang of the garment.

THE SAMPLER

All fabrics are worked in Rowan Botany Wool on TD 7, 40 R and 36 sts to 10cm (4in). Instructions are simplified and given for the number of R in specific CY; e.g. 1B = K 1 R in B.

Yarn color

A = navy, B = cream, C = gold, D = slate, E = red, F = green, G = pale green, H = pink, I = peach, J = pale blue, K = rust, L = pale yellow, M = mink

1 With A cast on and work as foll: 6A, 3B, 2C, 3B, 6A, 6D, 3B, 2E, 3B, 6D, 6A, 3B, 2F, 3B, 6A.

2 With A cast on and work as foll: 2A, 1B, 1J, 1F, 1I, 1K, 1C, 1D, 1L, 1E, 1H, 1C, 1A, 1K, 1L 1E, 1J, 1B, 1F, 1C, 1K, 1N, 1D, 1I, 1G, 1A, 1B, 1H.

3 With M cast on and work as foll: 4M, 1B, 2G, 1B, 4M, 4L, 1A, 2E, 1A, 4L, 4M, 1B, 2C, 1B, 4M, 4L, 1A, 2J, 1A, 4L, 4M, 1A, 2I, 1A, 4M.

4 With B cast and work as foll: 6B, 1C, 6G, 1H, 6B, 1D, 6G, 1E, 6B, 1I, 6G, 1A, 6B.

5 With A cast on and work as foll: 4A, 2L, 4A, 4B, 2J, 4B, 4A, 2K, 4A, 4B, 2F, 4B, 4A, 2L, 4A.

6 With B cast on and work as foll: 4B, 3I, 1J, 1B, 4F, 2B, 2C, 3B, 1E, 1K, 2B, 1A, 3L, 2B, 4J, 1B, 2F, 3B, 2E, 1B, 2C, 3B, 4A.

7 With A cast and work as foll: *1A, 1B, set carr to FM and take to opposite end 1A, 1B*. Now rep from * to * to end.

Welts With A cast on and work as foll: 9A TD 7, 1A TD 9, 2A TD 7, 2F, 2A, 2F, 1A. Hook up and bind off.

Sides With A cast on and work as foll: 9A TD 7, 1A TD 9, 2A TD 7, 2L, 5A. Hook up and bind off.

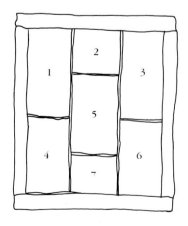

RAISED PATTERNS

There are several ways in which three-dimensional structures can be made on the single bed machine. This is a technique which must be controlled, perhaps more than any other, because wrongly used, it can look cheap and unsightly. The repeats of large raised sections and their position on the garment must be carefully considered so that they work stylistically, and are not unflattering.

The simplest way to create a raised effect on the single bed machine is to hook up. Hooking up at regular intervals produces a ripple fabric, like corrugated cardboard (3). This can be distorted by hooking up at different intervals to cause irregular waves (1), or staggered to produce a regular waved structure (4).

Welts are used repeatedly as a finish throughout machine knitting; the actual process of forming a welt can be used to make successful rippled fabrics. If you work them neatly at a sleeve head or in miniature for a neck detail, they can look very professional. Look at old linen with its ridges and ripples when considering scale. Be careful with large pleats; if they are not worked in a light yarn, they can be heavy and bulky.

Here the holding technique is used to achieve a three-dimensional effect (2 and 5). This can be used to add detail to the trims of a garment. Fabric 2 is interesting when worked the opposite way with the fullness at the edges. This creates a bow and would make a good detail on a collar. Fabric 7 is worked using a combination of hooking up and holding. This fabric would make a peplum, or can be used as a shaping method.

THE SAMPLER

All fabrics are worked with Rowan Botany Wool over 24 sts on TD 7 (unless otherwise stated), 40 R and 36 sts to 10cm (4in).

Yarn color

A = cream, B = yellow, C = peach, D = pastel green, E = gray, F = pink

1   With E cast on and K 4 R. Hook up a few sts at each end of work, not necessarily following R. K 4 R and hook up a few sts in the center of work. Cont in this way to cause a random effect. Alter the R in between slightly for more variety. K 4 R.

2   With D cast on and K 4 R. *Set carr to hold and put 6 sts on RT side to HP. K 1 R and put 6 sts at other edge to HP. K 4 R (over center sts only), return RT sts to WP. K 1 R, set carr to knit (to return others). K 2 R*. Rep from * to * 5 times. K 4 R.

3   With B cast on and K 4 R. *TD 10 K 1 R, TD 7 K 6 R. Hook up loose row. K 2 R*. Rep from * to * 9 times. K 4 R.

4   With C cast on and K 10 R. Count down at far LT edge 4 R and hook up 4 sts at LT edge from 4 R down. K 4 R and rep hook up, but this time 4 sts in, to form a regular diagonal ripple. Rep until you hook up at far RT edge, then hook up a 2nd ripple at LT edge as you form the last diagonal at RT edge to start a new R. After 4 diagonals have been made, K 4 R.

5   With A cast on and K 4 R. *TD 10 K 1 R. TD 7 K 10 R. Hook up from the loose row, 3 sts at each end and 4 in the center. K 2 R. TD 10 K 1 R. TD 7 K 10 R. Hook up from the loose row, 3 sts at each edge either side of the center 7 sts. K 2 R. *Rep from * to * twice. K 4 R.

6   With F cast on and K 4 R. *Set carr to hold and put 3 sts at each end and center 4 sts into HP. K 6 R, set carr to knit, K 2 R*. Rep from * to * 11 times. K 4 R.

7   (Fabric shown sideways.) With A cast on 30 sts and K 6 R. *Set carr to hold and mark RT side with thread, put LT 8 sts to HP and K 2 R*. Push 2 sts to HP and K 2 R. Rep this until only 12 sts rem in work, now hook up from the marker thread, put 2 sts back into WP on RT and K 2 R. Rep until only 8 sts are held, then hook up from marker thread a 2nd time. K 10 R*. Rep from * to * 7 times. K 6 R and bind off. If you do not hook up, the tucks can be sewn in after the knitting.

Welt   Hook up st for st and K 10 R str, TD 10 K 1 R, TD 7 K 4 R, TD 10 K 1 R, TD 7 K 5 R. Hook up from the loose row st for st and K 2 R. Rep this ripple once more, then K 2 R and hook up the main fabric st for st (you should be able to hook up your 1st R through the main fabric). K 1 R and bind off around the gate pegs.

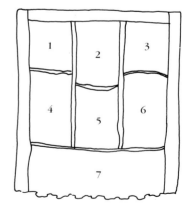

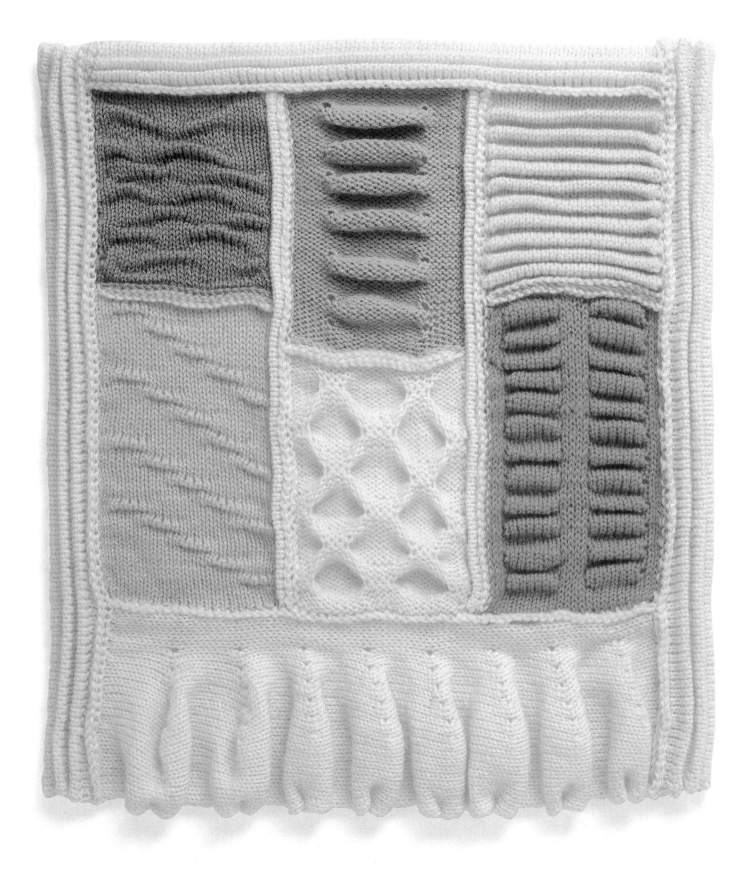

FAIR ISLE

Fair Isle is one of the most popular techniques in machine knitting. Two or more colors are used in one row to build up what looks like a complicated multi-colored pattern. It is very simple. Punchcards, or sheets on electronic machines, are used to tell the machine to select and knit certain needles. The fabric produced has floats across the back of the work, when knitted on a single bed machine.

Care must be taken when selecting yarns for Fair Isle on double bed machines. You don't want to be able to see different colored floats showing through the finished fabric. This can, however, be used to good effect if the yarns are different weights. Thicker yarn can be used to raise parts of the Fair Isle design.

When designing your Fair Isle, you will need to work within the limits of your machine. Stitch-related graph paper will help you achieve an accurate representation of the image

you want. Watch for the lengths of the floats; on commercial garments floats are seldom longer than 6 stitches. They tend to catch and distort the fabric otherwise. The number of colors you use in a row will be limited by your machine, but simple colorways are very effective.

Many machines have a switch which enables the card to be stopped and the rows to be selected twice – the same card can make several fabrics (3 and 7).

Fair Isle does not have to be used over the width of the whole garment. Some machines have a single motif facility which isolates a 24-stitch repeat. If you plan it carefully, your Fair Isle pattern can become a motif. Take care with the floats, which may cause distortion when selecting over a small area. When designing like this, work out your small repeat pattern on graph paper over a number of stitches that will divide equally into your repeat. For

example, if you are working on a 24-stitch repeat punchcard, you can work over 2, 3, 4, 6, 8 and 12 stitches, but make sure the design matches at the top and the bottom.

Once you have decided on the width of your repeat, the position of the design on the garment and the color sequences, you can punch your card. If you color your graph paper, you can do the color sequence straight from this rather than write out the pattern. If you do, make sure you color in an entire repeat, both width- and lengthways.

THE SAMPLER

All fabrics are worked in Rowan Botany Wool on TD 7, 40 R and 36 sts to 10cm (4in). Cast on 32 sts and work in st st from the punchcards (page 137). Fabrics 6, 7, 8 and 9 are shown upside down.

1 = punchcard 7
2 = Fair Isle punchcard 4
3 = punchcard 1 stopped
4 = punchcard 1 elongated (every R worked twice)
5 = Fair Isle punchcard 5
6 = punchcard 2
7 = punchcard 1
8 = Fair Isle punchcard 6
9 = punchcard 3

Welt Pick up st for st and K 9 R. Set Fair Isle punchcard 6 and work 4 R. Stop card and K 2 R st st. Hook up and bind off.

GAUGE PATTERNS

Interesting effects can be achieved by altering the tension, or stitch, dial while making any fabric. Fabrics can be accentuated by increasing the thickness or the number of ends of yarn used (note that you will have to loosen the gauge accordingly) or made less obvious by making the gauge differences less.

A change in the gauge either way causes a small ridge; this is useful for pleating. The godets on the short skirt (page 69) are formed with loose rows. Ladders and drop stitches also create pleats giving a lacy fabric. The more needles you leave out, the more lacy the fabric created by the floats and ladders.

Ladders are formed by leaving needles out of work so that the float is carried over to the next stitch, forming a ladder. Large amounts of stitches left out have to be transferred after the initial cast on for a neat finish. Drop stitches are stitches deliberately dropped during the knitting.

Leaving out needles is particularly convenient if you want to work by hand onto the fabric. Interesting stitches can be worked over "left" threads, and ladders also provide threading slots for ribbons or braids.

One of the most useful aspects of gauge is to indent, or raise the fabric. It is easy to produce a horizontal rib effect (4) by forming stripes and changing the setting alternately. This is a trick that works on both sides of the work (3). The tighter stripe indents on the knit side of the work, and raises on the reverse, or purl side, of the work. If you loosen the gauge further over the larger stripes (2), a strongly ridged fabric is made. A loose row helps to accentuate stripes too (6).

I have cheated a little and added a fabric that is made by holding (1). This gives you the opportunity to isolate tighter or looser areas of knitting.

THE SAMPLER

All fabrics are worked with Rowan Botany Wool, on TD 7 (unless otherwise specified), 40 R and 36 sts to 10cm (4in). Instructions are simplified and given for the number of R in a specific CY; 4A = K 4 R in A.

Yarn color

A = cream, B = rust, C = yellow, D = green, E = bright blue, F = red, G = mustard, H = black, I = pink

1   With A cast on and K 4 R, set carr to hold and push RT 12 N to HP. TD 10 K 1E, TD 7, set carr to knit, K 4A. Put 6 N at each end of work to HP. Set carr to hold, TD 10, K 1G, set carr to knit, TD 7 K 4A. Put LT half of N to HP, set carr to hold, TD 10 K 1B on rem sts. Cont to work in this way foll col sequence – the number of sts the loose R is worked over is shown in brackets. 4A, 1 × H (over RT 8), 4A, 1 x E (over LT 8), 4A, 1C, (over RT 16), 4A, 1D, (over center 8), 4A, 1F (over 8 at each end), 4A.

2   With A cast on and K 4 R TD 7, * TD 10 K 4F, TD 4 K 2A, 2C, 2A *. Rep from * to * foll col sequence and number of R: 4D, 2A, 2H, 2A, 4E, 2A, 2G, 2A, 4C, 2A, 2E, 2A, 4F, 4A. Bind off.

3   With A cast on * and K 8 R, TD 4 K 2F, 2H, 2F*. Rep from * to * foll col sequence and number of R: 8A, 2D, 2H, 2D, 8A, 2C, 2H, 2C, 8A, 2G, 2H, 2G, 8A, 2E, 2H, 2E, 8A.

4   With A cast on and K 2 R then trans every 6th st (3 × trans). K 4A, TD 10 K IH. TD 2 ∞ K 1H. Then work as foll: * TD 7, K 6A, TD 10 K 1C, TD 2 ∞ K 1C*. Rep this R and T sequence from * to * foll col sequence and number of R: 6A, 2F, 6A, 2D, 6A, 2B. Finish with 6A and bind off. Slip the ladder loop onto the empty N for a good bind-off edge.

5   With A cast on and K 2 R, trans every 4th st (5 x trans) and work as foll: *TD 7 K 4 R, TD 10 K 1 R*. Rep from * to * 6 times (7 in total). TD 7 K 4 R.

6   (Fabric shown sideways.) With A cast on * and K 6 R. TD 3 K 4B*. Rep from * to * foll col sequence A, C, A, D, A, E, A, F, A, G, A, I. K 6A.

Pleated edge   Cast on in A for the length of the pleat, TD 7 K 10 R, TD 9 K 1 R, *TD 7 K 10 R, TD 9 K 1 R, TD 7 K 20 R, TD 9 K 1 R.* Rep from * to * until the required number of pleats is worked.

Welt   Pick up st for st. TD 5 K 5 R. TD 7 K 1 R. TD 5 K 5 R. Hook up and bind off.

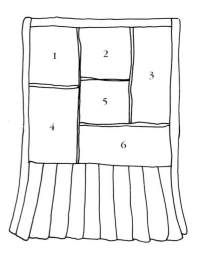

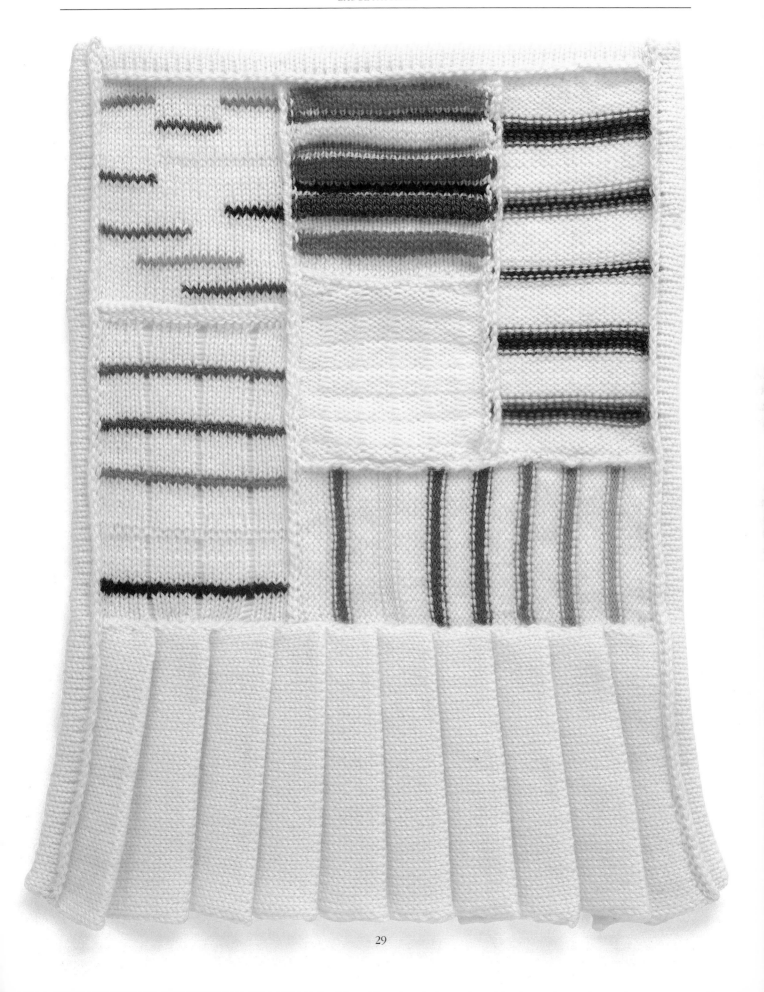

TUCKING

In a tuck stitch the yarn is laid over the hook of the needle which is to be tucked within the pattern. It is not knitted, but left with the stitch from the previous row and both are treated as one stitch on the next row. This creates a textural effect dependant on the needles selected to be tucked. This is all done automatically and the punchcard selects the needles to be tucked; it can be done manually too (6).

Normally stitches are tucked singly. This is because tucking four together would tangle up the machine; the loop would be too big. So when designing tuck fabrics, keep one knit stitch between the stitches to be tucked. There are exceptions. You can tuck with two needles together (5).

Tucking always makes the work wider. For example, if you cast on the same amount of stitches and work one sample in stockinette stitch and one in tuck stitch, the tuck stitch sample will be wider. You can get raised effects with tuck (3). The more rows you tuck, the more texture you will achieve, although the amount of times you tuck in succession is limited.

THE SAMPLER

All fabrics are worked in Rowan Botany Wool, TD 7, 40 R and 36 sts to 10cm (4in). Fabrics 2 and 5 can only be done on machines that double the length of card and repeat the pattern. Punchcards on page 137.

Yarn color

A = cream, B = red, C = green, D = slate, E = gray, F = yellow

1 Cast on 20 sts in A and K 4 R. Set machine to K tuck st using punchcard 3. K 4 R E, then K 4 R A until R 50.

2 Cast on 22 sts in A and K 4 R. Set machine to K tuck st using punchcard 7 set to L. *K 4 R A and K 4 R F.* Rep from * to * with col sequence A, D, A, B, A, C, A, F.

3 Cast on 20 sts in A and K 4 R. Set machine to K tuck st using punchcard 2. K 2 R A and K 2 R F until R 50.

4 Cast on 20 sts in A and K 4 R. Set machine to K tuck st one way and knit the other way using punchcard 1. Work 2 R D and 2 R A until R 50. K 4 R.

5 Cast on 22 sts in A and K 10 R. Set machine to K tuck st using punchcard 7 set to L. Push 7 N at each end to HP but do not set machine for hold. These 7 N will K st st but the center 8 will K tuck st. Rep this R 24 times, then K 10 R st st.

6 Cast on 20 sts in A and K 4 R. Set machine to K tuck st using punchcard 1 stopped. Work 2 R tuck with C and 2 R st st with A until R 50. K 4 R.

7 Cast on 20 sts in A and K 4 R. Set machine to hold and push ev 3rd N to HP, K 2 R F. Set machine to knit back from HP, K 2 R st st A. Rep these 4 R until R 50.

8 Cast on 20 sts in A and K 4 R. Set machine to K tuck st using punchcard 1 stopped. *Work 2 R tuck in F and 2 R A st st*. Rep from * to * in col sequence as foll: D, A, B, A, C, A, F, A to R 46. K 4 R in A. (Reverse shown.)

9 Cast on 20 sts in A and K 4 R. Set machine to K tuck st using punchcard 2. K 2 R A and K 2 R D until R 50. (Reverse shown.)

Welt   Pick up st for st and K 16 R. Hook up and bind off.

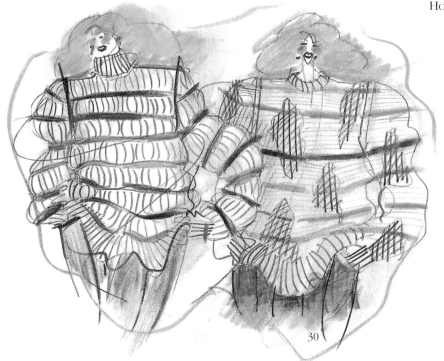

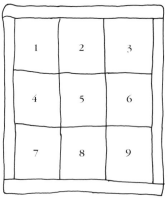

HAND TEXTURE

For the owner of a single bed domestic machine, hand texture provides endless possibilities for rib structures and purl stitch details. For those with a ribber attachment, these patterns can be worked by transferring from the back bed to the front bed, working one row and transferring back again, following the chart. Cables can be set into purl channels; purl stitch edgings can be worked while shaping. Many handknitting qualities can be introduced to your machine knitting in this way.

Traditional fishermen's knitting is a perfect source for ideas on hand texture. The gansey suit (page 102) was based on a fishermen's gansey. If you collect postcards and old books you will sometimes be able to see the stitches clearly enough to work from their patterns.

The basis of hand texture is making a purl loop on the right side of the work with a hand tool. It may seem laborious, but it is simple to do, and you do have greater control and can see the structure and how it is formed. This is most useful as it will also help you to mend your fabric and pick up dropped stitches. The rib detail on the lacy inset of the T-shirt (page 66) and the gansey suit motifs and detailing are examples of hand texture work.

There are machine accessories available that will do this. The garter carriage forms the stitches, whereas the transfer lock automatically transfers stitches.

Moss stitch is one of the most popular stitches (3 and 7). Motifs work well in moss stitches (5). It is best to graph them out first, using stitch-related graph paper if possible. The fabric in the center of the sampler, for example, has initials knitted-in with purl stitch. Useful graphs for lettering can be found in embroidery books, although they will not be stitch related, so alter them accordingly.

THE SAMPLER

All the pattern details are given for the dimensions of the sampler. All fabrics are worked in Rowan Botany Wool on TD 7, 40 R and 36 sts to 10cm (4in).

Yarn color
A = cream, B = red, C = yellow, D = green, E = slate

Cast on 24 sts and work from the charts on page 134. Each filled square represents a purl stitch on the right side of the fabric. The monogrammed fabric in the center of the sampler has no graph for the initials; you can insert your own.

1 = 2 × 2 rib in E
2 = horizontal rib in A
3 = single moss stitch in B
4 = checks in A
5 = insert your own monogram in purl stitches on a background of stockinette stitch in A
6 = seeded rib in A (reverse shown)
7 = double moss stitch in C
8 = 3 × 1 rib in A (reverse shown)
9 = diagonal rib in D

Welt Pick up st for st and K 16 R. Hook up and bind off.

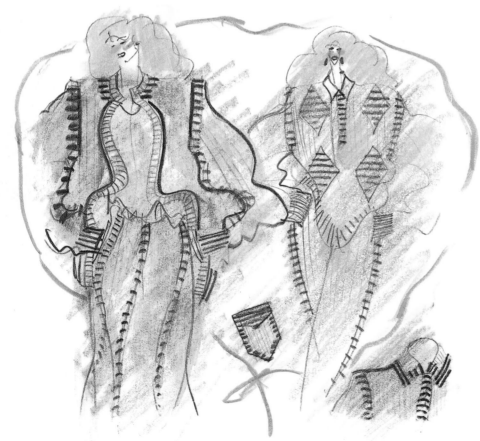

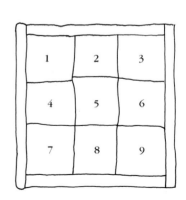

HOLDING

Holding, or partial knitting, enables the knitter to leave selected needles and their stitches out of work while knitting on the others. This is the way you knit a circle (5), by knitting more at one edge than the other.

When using holding it is also possible to produce a good intarsia imitation (3 and 4). The designs are obviously more limited than real intarsia but it is suitable for geometric and less figurative work.

Holding is the technique used to shape necklines, sleeve caps and shoulders. If you shape a shoulder by putting needles into HP, this means that you can work one row across all stitches at the shoulder giving a straight edge, rather than the steps that are produced by binding off at the beginning of every row.

If you put the needles in and out of HP and knit in the loops that are formed over the needles, you can form a sort of bound effect (7). Make these lines at least 8cm (3in) away from each other or you will have problems getting the weight in the correct position when the stitches tend to rise up. Make sure that the yarn is not too thick – no thicker than 4-ply and no more than 6 stitches on HP at one time.

THE SAMPLER

All fabrics are worked in Rowan Botany Wool, TD 7, 40 R and 36 sts to 10cm (4in). Dimensions are given for fabrics shown.
Punchcards on page 137.

Yarn color
A = cream, B = slate, C = red, D = green, E = yellow, F = gold

1   Using A cast on 28 sts and K 6 R st st. Set machine to hold. Push 6 sts to LT of center and 14 sts to RT of center to HP and K 6 R in A, 10 R in D, 12 R in A. Push these N to HP and push center 12 N to WP. K 4 R in A, 2 R in B, 10 R in A, 6 R in E, 6 R in A. Push

these N to HP and push 8 N at RT to WP. K 8 R in A, 8 R in C, 12 R in A, K 4 R st st in A over all N.

2   Using A cast on 26 sts and K 2 R. Bring to HP ev 7th needle and set machine to hold. K 1 R. *Bring forward to HP next N to LT of each held N, K 1 R*. Rep from * to * 2 times more. Change to D. **Bring first N on RT of each set of 4 N in HP to WP and place loops into hook of the N. K 1 R.** Rep from ** to ** with next N to RT of held N. Rep until all sts are back to WP. Change to A, K 2 R. Rep the whole procedure using the col sequence C, A, F, A, B, A.

3   Using A cast on 29 sts and K 4 R. Set machine to hold. Push all N to LT of center to HP. Using D push 1 N to HP at the center on ev R until all N are in HP. Complete in the same way for all N to RT of center but using E. Using A push 1 N at center to WP and K 1 R. Push 1 N at each side of the center to WP on ev R until all N are in WP. Push 1 N to HP at each end of ev R until all N are in HP. Using C push 1 N at RT to WP on ev R until all N to RT of center are in WP. Push these N to HP and work over N to LT in the same way using B. K 4 R A over all N.

4   Cast on 28 sts and K 4 R. Set machine to hold and push all N to HP except for N 22 to 27 at LT, K 8 R D. Push these N to HP and select a further 6 N to WP, K 8 R C. Set machine to knit and K 8 R in A. Cont in this way making squares of col.

5   Cast on 16 sts with WY and K a few R. Join in A and set machine to hold. Push 1 N to HP at LT on ev R until all N are in HP. Push 1 N back from HP at RT on ev R until all N are in WP. Cont in this way but changing CY each time until the shaping has been repeated 4 times. Put sts onto WY. Pick up 2 sets of sts from WY, K 1 R.

6   Cast on 28 sts and K 4 R. Set machine to hold. Working in 2 R stripes in A and E, push 1 N to HP at LT on ev R until all N are in HP. Put in punchcard 1 to K Fair Isle and K with A and D. Push 1 N to WP at RT on ev R until all are in WP. Then push 1 N at LT to HP on ev R until all N are in HP. Working in 2 R stripes using A and B, push 1 N at LT to WP on ev R until all N are in WP. K 4 R in A.

7   Using A, cast on 29 sts and K 16 R. Set machine to hold. Push 1 N to HP at each end of ev R until all N are in HP. K 2 R in B over all N. Push all N to HP except center N. K 1 R in A. Push 1 N to WP each side of center on ev R until all N are in WP. K 16 R.

8   Using A cast on 26 sts and K 4 R. Set machine to hold. Bring forward 2nd N from LT to HP. K 1 R, bring out 3rd N from LT to HP. K 1 R. Bring 4th N from LT to HP, K 1 R. *Return first held N to WP, placing loops into hook of the N, bring out next N to RT of those held to HP. K 1 R.* Rep from * to * striping the foll R in col sequence: R 9-10 in D, R 19-20 in F, R 29-30 in C. When 3 N reach the edge of work, cont working as before but return N to WP. When all N are in WP, rep starting with 2nd N from LT.

Welt   Pick up st for st and K 16 R. Hook up and bind off.

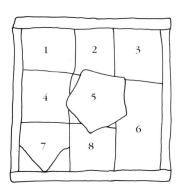

LACE

Lace fabrics are very attractive and provide infinite possibilities with attractive results. Beginners should not be put off by the complex appearance of these fabrics as they are often simple to knit.

You can pick up a lot about the design of knitted lace fabrics by looking at real lace. Details are important when working on such intricate pieces, so obtain reference to work from – a paper doily, a strip of lace, or a lace collar from a blouse.

Carriages that are used to transfer stitches are a great help for lace knitting. A lace carriage pre-selects the lace area and automatically transfers the stitches. Punching your own cards for them can be a bit complicated if you are a beginner, so in the sampler I have hand transferred all the fabrics for the benefit of those who do not own lace carriages. Also, it is better to hand transfer during fabric development because it saves time punching cards for designs which may not ultimately be suitable. Obviously for an all-over lace pattern, hand selection would be too time consuming.

To produce an eyelet or a one-lace hole, you need only transfer one stitch sideways and place it over the stitch on the next needle, leaving the empty needle in work position to pick up on the next row. When this is done with a multi-prong tool it will result in an interesting wale deflection which is often used in the construction of lace designs.

It is also possible to produce a lacy effect by dropping stitches (page 46). Here the dropped stitches make a ladder to form a check (1). You can vary the shape of the ladder by putting empty needles out of work. This is most effective when the transfer is done with a multi-prong tool. You then introduce the needles back in, forming a shaped ladder.

A row of eyelet holes is the basis for a picot edge, seen here as an edging to the sampler. The holes can be distanced further apart to achieve a small scallop-look edge.

Lace can be used to form motifs (5). It is best to chart designs first, as you would a Fair Isle motif, so that you don't waste time knitting inaccurate shapes. Obviously you can reverse the fabrics and form a plain motif on a lace base. Other stitches, such as moss stitch, hand texture, or cables can also be introduced.

Mesh fabric (7) is formed by transferring every other stitch, working two rows and transferring in the same way again, but moving along one stitch so that you transfer the stitch in between the eyelets below. This is a versatile fabric, and not as see-through as you might imagine.

If you work the lace inset within a plain knitted area, this will give the fabric a good edge; transferring in both directions alternately will prevent the work from "spiraling", which is a technical term used to describe the twisting action of the fabric. This occurs when working with tightly spun yarns or when transferring stitches continually in one direction. When working lace in a garment, it is a good idea to work the edge in stockinette stitch, to provide you with a neat, stable edge to make the seam. Some new machines will do this automatically.

Because lace provides holes, it is ideal for threading ribbons and other materials. The same technique can be used when you need a drawthread to gather up cuffs or necks. Buttonholes can be formed from eyelets, though only for small buttons.

THE SAMPLER

All fabrics are worked in Rowan Botany Wool in cream, on TD 7, 40 R and 36 sts to 10cm (4in). The lace patterns have been written in the form of charts (page 133).

1   (Fabric shown sideways.) Cast on 24 sts and K 4 R. Work from chart 1. Rep the sequence 3 times.

2   (Fabric shown sideways.) Cast on 24 sts and K 4 R. Work from chart 2. Rep the sequence 4 times.

3   (Fabric shown sideways.) Cast on 27 sts and K 4 R. Work from chart 3. Rep from beg to R 8. K 6 R.

4   Cast on 24 sts and K 4 R. Work from chart 4. Rep sequence 4 times. K 4 R.

5   Cast on 34 sts, K 4 R and work from chart 5.

6   Cast on 24 sts and K 4 R. Work from chart 6. Rep sequence twice (2nd time omitting center hole) but omit row 1 each time.

7   Cast on 26 sts and K 4 R. Work from chart 7. Rep sequence once.

8   (Fabric shown sideways.) Cast on 32 sts and K 4 R. Work from chart 8. Rep 20 R but alternate patt by starting chart 11 sts in from RT edge of chart.

9   Cast on 25 sts, K 4 R and work from chart 9. Rep from beg to R 10. K 4 R st st.

Edging   Pick up st for st, K 6 R and make a row of eyelet holes. K 6 R.

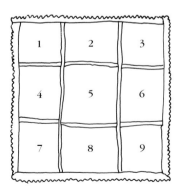

SLIP STITCH

Slip stitches are formed exactly as the name suggests, by skipping stitches. In handknitting this is referred to as slipping a stitch. The yarn which is not knitted is carried across the reverse of the work much like floats in Fair Isle fabrics. Because not all stitches are knitted on every row, the fabric produced is often denser and because of the floats, it will not stretch as much as a fabric like stockinette stitch, for example. Some of the structures (1 and 4) resemble holding and Fair Isle fabrics. Three-dimensional qualities can be achieved. The raised areas on fabric 3 are on the reverse side of fabric 9.

Slipping provides a method of achieving a one-row stripe effect automatically (6 shows the reverse side of this structure). The basic shirt alternative fabric (page 74) was done using the free move facility. This produces a more definite stripe and takes longer.

When designing your own slip stitch patterns, you must remember not to make large floats that could snag. If you must make large floats, they can be crocheted up the back of the work after knitting if you are using the knit side of the work. Or you can use the crocheted side and make the crochet stitches part of the fabric's structure.

THE SAMPLER

All fabrics are worked in Rowan Botany Wool, TD 7, 40 R and 36 sts over 10cm (4in). Cast on in A. Punchcards on page 137.

Yarn color
A = cream, B = red, C = yellow, D = green, E = slate

1   Cast on 20 sts and K 4 R. Set machine to K slip st using punchcard 1 stopped. Work 2 R E in slip st and 2 R A st st until R 50. K 2 R st st.

2   Cast on 28 sts and using A K 4 R. Set machine to slip st but with no punchcard. Push 2 N to UWP with 6 N in between and K 1 R with D. Rep this R 4 times then K 4 R st st with A. Cont until R 40 but changing the sets of sts in UWP to alternate with previous sets.

3   Cast on 24 sts and K 4 R. Set carr to K slip st with punchcard 1 stopped. *K 2 R st st. K 10 R slip A. Change to C. K 2 R st st. K 10 R slip,* rep from * to * in col sequence: A, E, A, B, A, D. K 4 R st st.

4   Cast on 20 sts and K 4 R. Set machine to slip st using punchcard 8. K 2 R slip D and K 2 R slip A until R 50. K 4 R st st.

5   Cast on 28 sts and K 4 R. K 18 R st st. Push all N, except the center 8, to UWP and set carr to slip, K 1 R. Rep this R 10 times then K 18 R st st.

6   Cast on 28 sts and K 4 R. Set machine to K slip st with punchcard 8. K 2 R slip A, K 2 R slip E until R 36. K 4 R st st. Reverse side shown here.

7   Cast on 28 sts and K 4 R. Set machine to K slip using punchcard 2 stopped . *Work 2 R slip st C. K 2 R st st A*. Rep from * to * K 4 R st st in A.

8   Cast on 28 sts and K 12 R A. Set machine to K slip but with no punchcard. Push 2 sets of 4 sts to UWP and K with D for 4 R. K 4 R st st with A and then rep changing sets of sts in UWP to alternate with previous R. K 4 R with C. Cont in this way using B and E. K 6 R in A.

9   Cast on 24 sts and K 4 R. Set machine to K slip st with punchcard 1 stopped. *K 2 R st st, K 10 R slip A. Change to B, K 2 R st st, K 10 R slip.* Rep from * to * 6 times. K 4 R.

Welt   Pick up st for st and K 16 R. Hook up and bind off.

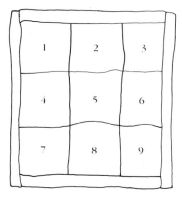

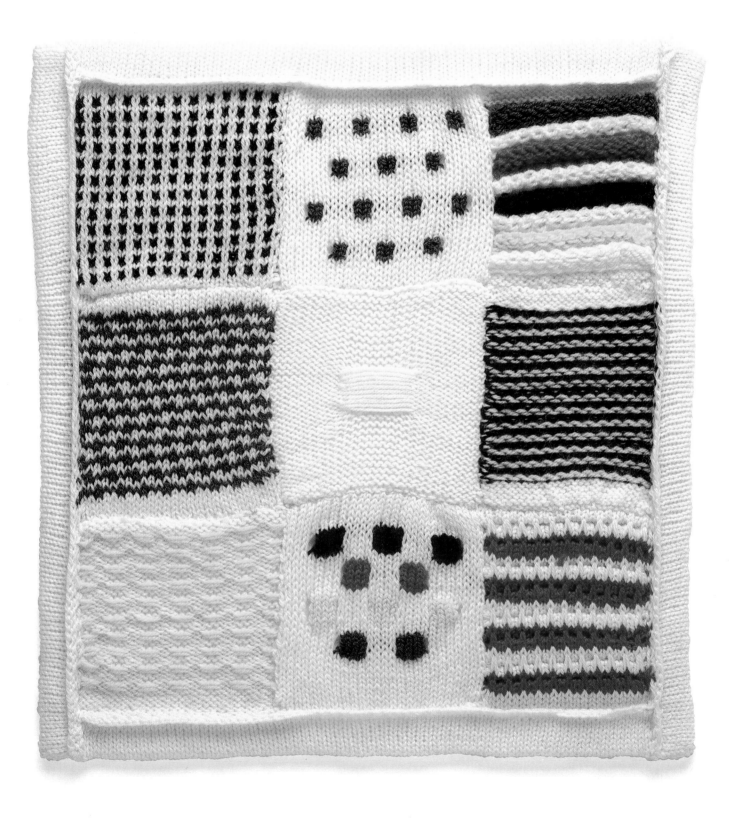

CABLES

Cables are formed by crossing over stitches and putting them onto the needles that have just been emptied on the opposite side (page 127).

You may find that you have trouble stretching the stitches when you are working with yarns which are not inclined to stretch, such as cotton and linen, or when working on a tight gauge. To some extent you will have to compromise with and slacken off a little more than you might normally. Another method of loosening the stitch is known as robbing yarn – stealing yarn to make the loops, or stitches, big enough so that they can be transferred. When you work several cables, they will rob yarn from each other, so it is a good idea to do a big sample for multi-cable pieces to check the final effect. When working out your cable pattern, you must also allow for shrinkage – not as in washing but in the technical sense of the word – especially if you are latching up afterwards. In effect you are creating a rib structure which will tend to shrink in.

The simplest method of gaining slack is to leave needles out of work so that a float is left, which is then taken up into the loop when it is transferred. This also gives the opportunity to latch up the remaining loops on the wrong side of the work forming a purl channel either side of the cable, as in hand and double bed knitting.

Extra slack can be gained by casting on only with the needles that will not be latched, then introducing the left-out needles into the work for the row before cabling so that they knit and take up more yarn. They can then be dropped and will not run beyond the point where you introduced them because they were actually knitted. This will produce a bigger loop, providing more scope for a larger transfer.

Holding is most useful when large transfers have to be made. If you knit short rows onto one side of the cable (or both) forming extra fabric to allow for the stretch, transfers will be easy and a three-dimensional effect will be possible. You will sometimes need to use a separate thread for this purpose.

THE SAMPLER

All fabrics are worked in Rowan Botany Wool in cream on TD 7, 40 R and 36 sts to 10cm (4in). When cabling, make sure the same sts are cabled behind each time. Fabrics 1, 3 and 4 are shown upside down.

1   Cast on 27 sts. K 6 R, and work as foll: *With 2 trans tool, cable sts 4 and 5 with sts 6 and 7. Skip 1 st and rep to end of R leaving 2 sts. K 2 R.* Rep from * to * 9 times. K 6 R.

2   (Fabric shown sideways.) Cast on 24 sts and K 6 R. Work as foll: * With 2 trans tool, cable sts 3 and 4 with st 5 (on 1 trans tool). Skip 2 sts. Rep to end of R leaving 2 sts. K 4 R.* Rep from * to * 6 times more. K 6 R.

3   Cast on 24 sts. K 6 R. Work as foll: *Cable sts 1 and 2 with st 3, skip 3 sts. Rep to end of R leaving 3 sts. K 4 R. Cable sts 5 and 6 with st 4. Skip 3 sts. Rep to end of R. K 4 R.* Rep from * to * 5 times then K 4 R and work 1st cable R once more. K 6 R.

4   Cast on 26 sts and K 8 R. Work as foll: *Cable sts 4 and 5 with 6 and 7. Skip 2 sts and rep to end of R leaving 3 sts. K 4 R. Cable sts 4 and 5 with 2 and 3, skip 2 sts and rep to end of R. K 4 R.* Rep from * to * twice more, work 1st cable R once more. K 8 R.

5   Cast on 24 sts and K 6 R. Work as foll: *With 3 trans tool, cable sts 4, 5 and 6 with 1, 2 and 3. Skip 6 sts and rep to end of R. K 4 R. Cable sts 4, 5 and 6 with 1, 2 and 3, then cable sts 10, 11 and 12 with 7, 8 and 9, rep to end of R.* Rep from * to * twice more then rep 1st cable R once more. K 6 R.

6   (In this fabric the cable is worked alternate ways.) Cast on 26 sts, K 6 R. Work as foll: *Cable sts 7 and 8 with 5 and 6, skip 3 sts, rep to end of R leaving 4 sts. K 6 R. Cable sts 5 and 6 with 7 and 8, skip 3 sts, rep to end of R, leaving 4 sts. K 6 R.* Rep from * to * once more, work the 1st cable R once more. K 6 R.

7   Cast on 24 sts. K 8 R. Work as foll: *Cable sts 4, 5 and 6 with sts 1, 2 and 3, skip 3 sts and rep twice more. K 4 R.* Rep from * to * 8 times. K 4 R.

8   (Fabric shown sideways.) Cast on 24 sts. K 6 R and work as foll: *Cable sts 5 and 6 with 7 and 8, then cable sts 11 and 12 with 9 and 10, skip 2 sts and rep once more. K 8 R.* Rep from * to * 3 times. K 8 R.

9   Cast on 25 sts. K 6 R. Work as foll: *Cable sts 5 and 6 with 3 and 4, then cable sts 7 and 8 with 9 and 10, skip 3 sts and rep once more. K 4 R.* Rep from * to * 6 times more. K 8 R.

Edging   Cast on 8 sts and *work 10 R cabling sts 2, 3 and 4 with 5, 6 and 7.* Rep from * to * to required length. (The extra st at each end is so the detail can be seen after seaming.)

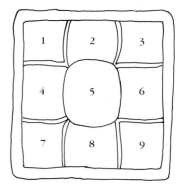

WEAVING

Weaving is a technique where a second yarn is caught into the work as it is being knitted. This produces a woven-looking fabric. The actual pattern in which the second yarn is woven is usually determined by a punchcard. You can produce areas of isolated weaving (8), thus producing an effect similar to intarsia, as in the carpet jacket (page 110) and wrap (page 83).

Weaving is most useful for thickening up fabrics and heavier yarns can be used because they are trapped into the work rather than actually taken through the hook of the needle.

When working with a number of different colors in this way, it is easier to place cones on the floor and work with short lengths where the area to be filled is small. This is done by laying the weaving yarn over the needles that you wish to weave in on (at random or following a graph) and working as normal. Owners of non pre-selecting machines should use hand selection for this. This is obviously more involved and time-consuming, but with the help of a needle pusher, the more geometric designs should not take too long.

THE SAMPLER

All fabrics are worked in Rowan Botany Wool TD 7, 40 R and 36 sts to 10cm (4in). Cast on 24 sts in A unless otherwise stated.
Punchcards on page 137.

Yarn color
A = cream, B = red, C = green, D = yellow, E = navy

1 K 2 R. Set machine to knitweave and punchcard 1. Weave 5 R with 2 ends of col seq A, B, A, C, A, D, E, A for 40 R.

2 K 4 R. Set machine to knitweave and punchcard 1. Weave 40 R with 2 ends of E.

3 K 4 R in D. Set machine to knitweave and punchcard 1. *Weave 12 R with 2 ends of A.* Leave center 16 sts to K st st, use 2 separate balls of A and weave only over outside sts for 16 R. Rep from * to *.

4 K 4 R. Set machine to knitweave and punchcard 1. With card locked on R 1, weave 40 R with 2 ends of E. Use reverse of fabric.

5 K 4 R. Set machine to knitweave and punchcard 2. Weave 40 R with 2 ends of B.

6 K 4 R. Set machine to knitweave and punchcard 1. Lay 1 end of C and B over 3 hand-selected N at each end to form a diamond. Change to D and E.

7 K 4 R. Bring every other N to UWP and e-wrap C over these empty N. K across R, select alt N not used before and e-wrap again. K 6 R A. Rep with CY in sequence B, D, E.

8 K 4 R. Set machine to knitweave and punchcard 1. Weave 20 R laying 2 ends of E over selected N to form a diamond.

9 K 4 R. Set machine to knitweave and punchcard 2. With card locked on R 1, weave 40 R with 2 ends of C. This is the reverse of fabric 5.

Welt Pick up st for st and K 16 R. Hook up and bind off.

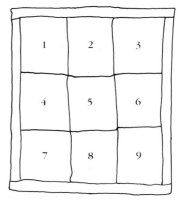

INTARSIA

This is a technique which enables the knitter to work freely with color or different yarns without floats at the back of the fabric. The only real restriction is the width of the machine. Any patterns and color mixtures are possible when working with this technique. Each color is taken back and forth within its shape and the yarns are crossed where they join to avoid a hole forming, as you would work in handknitting.

The basis of the technique is the laying over of yarn onto specific needles that make up the design. The sampler opposite is a variation on an Argyle design. Another thing to note about intarsia is that the reverse side looks the same as the right side.

You can either work with a random approach, excellent for impatient knitters, or for more figurative designs, graph out the image first. Owners of charting devices (page 140) can use them for intarsia.

When graphing out your design, it is important to work with stitch-related graph paper so that, as in Fair Isle design, the image is not distorted. Also, most importantly, if your design is not symmetrical and you plan to use stockinette stitch side of the work as the right side, intarsia charts should be worked in the reverse as though you were looking from the wrong side of the fabric (check your manual).

It is a good idea to work out approximately how much each area will need in yarn and separate these lengths of yarn out so that knitting is less complicated and neater. As there are no floats, each area, even those in the main yarn, needs a separate end of yarn. Neatness is essential when working in this way, especially if your design has a lot of colors in each row.

If you are not sure whether your machine will do intarsia or not, refer to your manual to check the settings needed. Basically you need the facility to knit a yarn laid over the needle and not taken through the carriage at the patterning position (UWP). You will find that even very old machines do intarsia, so experiment using the functions table on page 118 if you do not have a manual or there is no reference to intarsia in your manual.

Some machines have an intarsia carriage. This is a completely separate carriage which is smaller and less complex than the standard carriage. It is used solely for intarsia work. An intarsia effect can also be worked using the holding technique (page 34). This is quicker if your design is geometric but the designs are limited.

As well as different colors, different yarn thicknesses can be used in intarsia to create texture. Heavier yarns are used for defined areas in traditional Scottish intarsia, thus creating a slightly raised image. You could, for example, try cotton, silk, linen or flat yarns, with alpaca wool or chenille. This is an excellent way to use up odd bits of yarn; there is no limit to how small the shape can be, and you can tie different colors together to use as a single yarn, and leave the tie ends for texture. Because the yarns in intarsia are not fed through the machine, but are laid over by hand, the work is time-consuming, but interesting effects can be achieved.

THE SAMPLER

The fabric is worked in Rowan Botany Wool on TD 7, 40 R and 36 sts to 10cm (4in). The sampler is shown here sideways.
Cast on 72 sts and work from the chart on page 132.

Welt   Pick up st for st and K 9 R in MY. Then work 9 R from the chart. Hook up and bind off. Work other sides the same way. Follow the photograph for border color sequence.

DOUBLE BED TECHNIQUES

A double bed machine has two beds of needles, the second one usually referred to as a ribber on domestic machinery and a front bed in commercial terms.

Knitters who work on single bed machines have to put far more effort into achieving a professional finish. This is because they cannot produce a real rib automatically. The alternatives are to create purl stitches manually on the knit side of the work or to invest in a garter carriage.

Working with two beds forms the knit and purl loops automatically – in other words making a rib. This gives the knitter far more scope for creating fabrics, shaping, finishing and detail. All manner of effects can be achieved by combining different techniques with rib.

The second bed also offers the knitter techniques such as laying in, as well as extensions to existing techniques such as drop stitch. Useful structures, such as the ladder stop (page 121), save time and improve the finish.

Drop Stitch

This is a lacy type of fabric, which is often worked within a single bed structure. The needles from the opposite bed are introduced for several rows and then these stitches are dropped so that they run down the fabric (hence the name drop stitch), producing a loose area. The positions of these areas can be altered by either changing the needles which are selected to knit on the opposite bed (1), or by selecting the same needles each time but moving the opposite bed along (racking) when there are not any needles in work on it, thus staggering the pattern. Drop stitch can also be worked in rows by selecting all needles on the opposite bed, forming a horizontal line (4).

Lace

Lace fabrics can be most effective on double bed machines as both the purl and knit sides can be used with the lacy structures. The stitches are transferred from one needle to the next to form the eyelet holes of the lace.

You can use rib to accentuate the lacy inset panels (7). Attractive examples can be made using a single bed base and working the panels in double bed so that the lace pattern is raised up. This is similar to the relief technique.

Laying In

This technique looks very much like weaving on a single bed machine except the laid-in yarn is trapped between two sections of knitting. It is easy to do as long as you are careful to push the laid-in yarn well down between the two beds. Some machines will lay in automatically.

Cast on and knit tubular, then take a thicker yarn and put it into the tubular pocket you have formed. Now work at least one row on both beds to seal the pocket. This fabric can be made more interesting by leaving out needles on the front bed to cause a checked effect (3). Alternatively, move the needles in and out of work in regular or random patterns. Be careful that the gaps between the needles are not too great; the laid-in yarn will snag.

THE SWATCHES

Yarn color

All fabrics are worked in Rowan Botany Wool.
A = cream, B = green, C = gold, D = red, E = slate, F = yellow

1   Drop stitch

Cast on back bed only with A, TD 2, *work 8 R. Change to D and work 1 R. Change to F and bring in 3 N on front bed. Leave next 3 out. Rep to end of work. Set machine to half pitch. Work 1 R on both beds with F. Select to knit on front bed and non-knit on back bed. Drop the stitches from the front bed.* Rep from * to * changing CY.

2   Woven checks

Back bed all N in. Front bed ev other N × 3, 4 in, ev other N in × 3.

Cast on with A and work 4 R, both beds TD 3/4. *Set back TD to 5 and work 4 R back bed only in A. Place 6 ends of E in between the 2 beds. Push well down. TD 3/4. Work 1 R both beds in A.* Rep from * to * 9 times, working 6 ends of CY in col sequence E, D, E, E, B, E, E, F, E.

3   Laying in

Ev other N front bed, machine set at half pitch. All N back bed.
Cast on with A and work 6 R, both beds TD 3/4. *Set back TD to 5 and work 4 R back bed only in A. Place 6 ends of CY in between 2 beds. Push well down. TD 3/4. Work 1 R both beds in A.* Rep from * to * 8 times. K 6 R in A on both beds, TD 3/4.

4   Checked lace

Push back ev 5th N to NWP.
With A, cast on back bed, TD 3 work 8 R str. * Bring corresponding front bed N into action. Work 1 R. Knock off front bed (as for drop stitch). Change to D (on back bed), work 1 R, change to C, work 1 R, change to E, work 1 R, change to A, work 8 R str*. Rep from * to * twice changing CY. K 8 R.

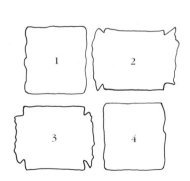

On double bed machines, effective results can be obtained by laying in with strips of leather. It is important to make sure that you lay them in neatly and that the strips are cut accurately for the best effects. Fine strips or thonging will knit, but you may find it better to knit with another yarn, such as mercerized cotton, and work a drop stitch structure, working the row to be dropped with the leather and the other rows with the cotton. This makes knitting much easier and enables you to work with slightly thicker strips.

Relief Knitting

This can be done in a number of ways. One way is for the relief to be formed by a purl stitch, transferring stitches to the front bed so that you get a damask effect. This is widely used commercially. Complex large repeat designs work well if graphed out first, but they are quite time-consuming to produce if you don't have a transfer carriage.

Textured images can be formed by starting off on the back bed, then introducing needles from the front bed – in other words working on a single bed base and forming shapes with double bed sections. These can be accentuated by tucking one way on the front bed; this gives you half cardigan, or half fisherman's rib, on a single bed base (5).

Color can be introduced on the back bed only to form a broken stripe, and the areas of double bed can be arranged so that they react against each other to cause wale deflection. However, you must be careful not to distort the fabric to the extent that it cannot be used for a garment.

Tucking

This is most effective on a double bed machine and the extra bed produces a much more substantial fabric (7). All the needles are used in this example, but interesting effects can be gained with a rib structure (page 125).

Cables

Because cables are normally set into ribs, they look more professional when worked on a double bed machine, but they can be tricky to transfer. The extra bed gives the knitter the opportunity to transfer more stitches further along the bed, because you can use the needles on the opposite bed to rob yarn on the previous row which makes the stitches bigger and easier to transfer. To rob yarn, needles which are out of work directly opposite the stitches to be cabled are put into work so that the yarn loops over them. This yarn is then released forming larger loops which can be transferred.

Purl Fabrics

Because it is possible with a double bed machine to produce a purl stitch and transfer stitches to give a purl fabric, it is also possible to reproduce purl-based stitches, such as moss stitch, by transferring one set of stitches from one bed to the other. Although slow, this process enables the knitter to introduce texture with all the other possibilities a double bed machine offers.

Finishes

Finishing is the area where owning a double bed machine really does give you an advantage. Real rib collars, trims and plackets attached with linking slots look very professional, and last longer. You can also make bindings and edgings and finish your work professionally, rather than being confined to the limits of single bed machinery.

THE SWATCHES

Yarn color

A = cream, B = green, C = gold, D = red, E = slate

5 Relief knitting

Cast on with A on both beds. Trans all sts onto back bed except 2 sts at each end. Set machine to tuck one way on front bed only. Introduce sts to front bed randomly ev R, then trans them to the back bed to produce vague diamond shapes. Rep the process forming the next set of diamonds between the first set. This fabric was worked at random; you could plan it on a chart beforehand.

6 Color relief knitting

Cast on with A. Trans sts to front bed randomly ev R, then bring sts back into work to produce diamonds. *Work 2 R in B front bed only, work 2 R in A both beds.* Rep from * to * working 4 stripes in D, 4 stripes in E, and so on in col sequence. The col sections in this sample are produced by working on one bed only with the CY, then working on both beds with the MY; thus working more R on the front bed.

7 Two-color tuck stitch

Cast on with A on both beds, approx TD 3/4, work 3 R. Set punchcard 1 (page 137) stopped on R 1. *Set machine to tuck st both ways and work 2 R in C. Set machine to knit, change to A. Work 2 R.* Rep from * to * 7 times, here shown with CY. Work 1 R in A.

8 Lace

Cast on 28 sts with A and trans 3 sts to back bed, leave 5 sts on front bed, 1 st on back bed, 5 sts on front bed, 3 sts on back bed, 5 sts on front bed. *Hand trans lace over center 5 sts and push center N to HP on 3 sts on back bed, K 4 R. K 2 R over all N*. Rep from * to *.

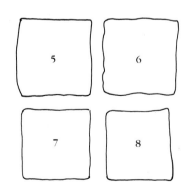

Roll Back Edging

One edging that is simple to make and attach is a roll back edging. This finish is often used commercially. You can attach this in several ways. One of the most useful is to tuck the edging under the edge to be finished and leave the roll edge curling back over. This gives a similar effect to the one used on the tailored suit (page 88).

Purl Edging

This is a fine, delicate edging that looks neat when attached with a linking machine (page 129) or when hand linked. It is simply a knitted strip with a row of purl stitches worked at the point where it bends. The binding can be attached and will fit easily around the edge because of the purl row. The only drawback with this edging is that the length of it is determined by the width of the machine so neat joins are essential.

Working Beds Independently

It is possible to work the beds independently of each other so that you work, for example, one color on the front bed and another on the back. This gives you a two-colored double fabric joined at the bottom. This is useful for linings or reversible garments. You can achieve a quilted look by transferring stitches from one bed to the other, thus joining the beds from time to time. Wadding could be added to make a thicker fabric.

This technique can also be used to form patches (10 and 11). Make sure that the weight is evenly distributed so the fabric doesn't ride up in knitting. This idea could be used to form a pocket.

THE SWATCHES

9   Purl edging

Cast on 28 sts TD 7 and K 10 R in WY. K 8 R MY and then trans all N to back bed and K 1 R. Trans all sts to front bed and K 8 R MY, K 10 R WY.

10   Squares

Cast on 28 sts TD 7 and K 4 R. On back bed bring into WP 6 N and K 1 R on both beds. Set machine to K only on front bed and K 8 R MY. Set machine to knit on back bed only and, with CY, K 8 R. Trans the sts to the front bed and select a further set of N on back bed and K 1 R on both beds. Cont in this way until R 40.

11   Roll back edging

Cast on 26 sts in a K1 P1 rib arrangement. K 1 R then trans 4 sts at LT to front bed so that N to RT are K1 P1 but 8 N at LT are st st. TD 4 K 34 R.

12   Triangle

Cast on 28 sts TD 7 and K 4 R. On back bed bring into WP 10 N and K 1 R on both beds. Set machine to knit only on front bed and K 8 R MY. Set machine to knit on back bed only and, with CY, K 8 R, dec 1 st using 3 trans tool at both edges ev alt R until 1 st remains. Trans this st to the front bed and cont working on front bed only.

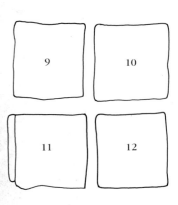

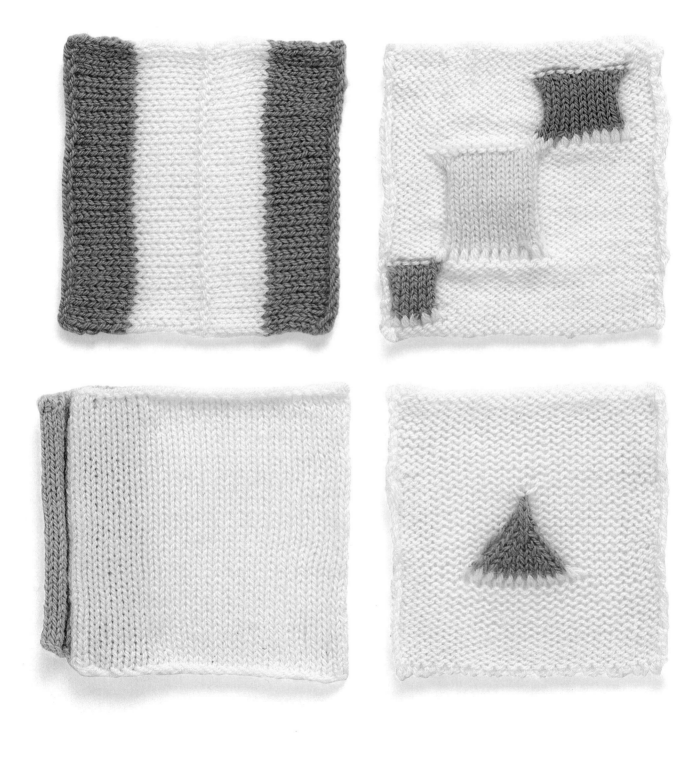

MIXING HAND & MACHINE TECHNIQUES

There are many ways to create interesting fabrics and garment finishes by mixing hand and machine knitting. Because it is a loose fabric, it is simple to hook handknitting onto the machine as you work. This provides a good joining method for the two types of work and saves time sewing up later. Hooking on sections as you work is a useful and versatile technique for finishing pockets and patches, for example.

If you are inserting a panel of handknitting (2), you must allow stitches on the handknitted piece for hooking on at the edges. Isolate part of the handknit pattern, write it out first so that you don't get confused and then add on the extra stitches. When you have made your handknit piece, it is a good idea to do a sample to see how many rows you need to work between "hook ons." Cast on with your machine and work up to the point where you wish to add the inset, hook the first part on (with the right side facing you) and work as many rows as it takes to get to your next hook-on point. This test will help you assess the ratio of rows to hook ups; normally you would hook up every one to four rows, but if you are working with an irregular shape you may find that you have to do it by eye, or do a complete test first.

The major advantage of using handknitting for the single bed machine owner is ribbing. Bottom ribs can be worked by hand first and hooked onto the machine, then the bodies worked onto them. Collars (1) and real rib trims make such a difference and look more professional.

Even large pieces of handknitting can be added to machine knits. A Fair Isle sweater can be made by working a plain machine-knit body and sleeves up to the yoke level, putting work onto waste yarn and picking the stitches up (thus joining all the pieces together), and then working the yoke on top by hand. You do not even have to work out the handknit yoke; just find a pattern and match up the gauge, rows and stitches on your machine knitting to the handknit pattern, or use a chart device. Use the size of needle to match the machine gauge.

If you wish to add a rib into the waist of a garment, work the first section from the hem to the waist, then take the work off onto waste yarn and pick up the stitches on knitting needles to work the ribbing. When ribbing is complete, return the work to the machine and continue knitting.

THE SWATCHES

All fabrics are worked in Rowan Botany Wool on TD 7, 40 R and 36 sts to 10cm (4in).

1 Collar
Pick up st for st around neck (using No. 1/2.75mm needles; a circular needle is best) and work the ribbing stitch. This swatch has been knitted in twisted K1 P1 rib, working into the back of every K st. Inc 1 st at each end of every alt R. Bind off when desired width of collar is reached.

2 Inset
Pattern details are given for the dimensions of this swatch.
MY = cream, CY = green
Using MY and No. 1/2.75mm needles, cast on 16 sts and work 5cm (2in) as foll:
Row 1 * P1 yb, sl 1 p-wise, yfwd*, rep from * to *.
Row 2 P.
Row 3 Using CY yb, sl 1 p-wise, yfwd P1*, rep from * to *.
Row 4 P.
On machine, cast on 28 sts, TD 7, using e-wrap method and MY. K 10 R. Pick up and place 16 sts from cast-on edge of handknitted piece evenly onto 12 N at center. Bind off tog. Push all N to LT to HP. K 20 R on N at RT, picking up 1st st from edge of hand-knitted piece and placing it onto N 13 ev R. Push these N to HP and work in the same way on N at LT. Pick up 16 sts from cast-off edge of handknitted piece and place evenly onto center 12 N. K 10 R over all N.

3 Crochet edge
Crochet is a useful form of hand work for adding detail and finishing to a machine-made work. A couple of rows of a simple stitch like slip stitch or single crochet will prevent an edge from rolling back.

With the RT side facing, and a crochet hook approx the same gauge as the N, work evenly around the edge. The intervals between the stitches must be consistent or there will be distortion.
red = slip stitch (page 129)
gold = picot edge (page 129)
Join the yarn to the knitting with a sl st, *4 ch, 1 sl st into next st*. Rep from * to * along edge.
green = single crochet (page 129)
slate = button holes
Join the yarn to the knitting with a sl st, *3 sc, 6 ch*. Rep from * to * along edge.

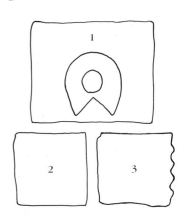

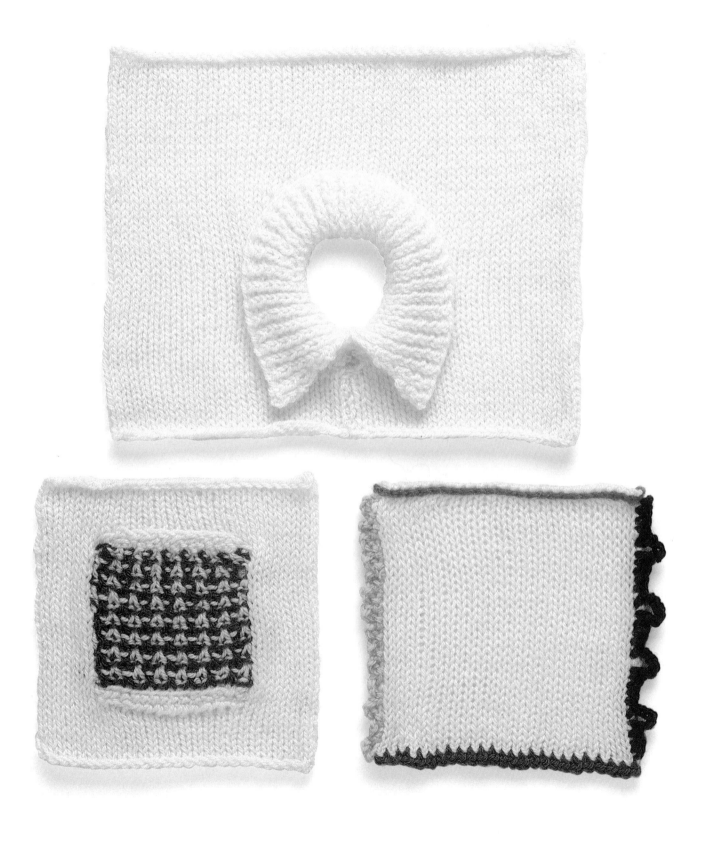

STRETCHING YOUR MACHINE

There is far more to your knitting machine than those techniques outlined in the manual and you should explore your machine's full potential. It is understandable that you might be apprehensive about developing fabrics on the machine. This is usually because you feel that you have not got the confidence to overcome disasters which may make you lose concentration. It is important to make the machine work for you; this is a good way of finding out how it functions.

Hand texture is covered on page 32, and although it can be laborious, it is a good example of how you can stretch your machine. Another method of producing purl loops on the right side of the fabric without a garter carriage or ribber is to put your work onto waste yarn, turn it around and put it back onto the machine. This is obviously more useful for large areas like yokes or stripes.

When working with hand texture, you see the purl side of the fabric and form knit loops. The turning technique enables you to go from purl base with knit loops to knit base with purl loops in a fraction of the time. Turning is also useful for pleats; a row of purl makes a perfect fold in the fabric. Double-bed knitters only have to transfer from one bed to another to do this.

Pre-knitting pieces and adding them on as you knit (page 52) speeds things up considerably. Pockets can be grafted onto the garment as it is knitted and sleeves set in the same way (1). This looks neat, secures the fabric with a stretch stitch and saves a lot of time as the garment is nearer to completion when it is taken off the machine. Knit your pocket first and then work the body pieces up to where the pocket is to be positioned.

Be careful to work out this positioning. A mistake will mean reknitting the whole thing. Next hook on the pocket stitch for stitch. Work two rows and take the next large loop up the side of the pocket and place on the same needle. Repeat until the pocket is secured.

Make sure you remember to knit your pieces in the correct order so that you have the relevant piece to hook on. This usually means doing the sleeves and trims first. This process is also useful for grafting together pieces of fabric when larger widths are required. The wrap (page 83) could be worked in this way.

If you want to work shapings at both edges of work in one direction, for example, in a continuous diagonal where you may only work over 60 stitches, you may run out of needles because you are continuously moving across the machine. A way to overcome this problem is simply to transfer back, or put the work onto waste yarn, remove it from the machine and move it back along the needles.

When used in the correct way, moving down the machine in this way enlarges the bed significantly and is most useful when binding off together on very long seams. Simply hook onto the full bed, bind off the stitches, then enlarge the last loop, remove from the machine, move it back the required number of needles and finish the bind off. You will have an extra end if you work a row before the seaming, but this can easily be sewn in to the back of work.

Moving is useful in conjunction with holding and shaping. This enables you to work enormous pieces of fabric. This is done by continually hooking on as you work (as above) but shaping the pieces so that they interlock (2).

THE SWATCHES

All fabrics are worked in Rowan Botany Wool, TD 7, 40 R and 36 sts over 10cm (4in).

1   To make a seamed piece, K fabric in MY (cream). Cast on sts in CY and pick up 1 st on ev R from the bound off edge of MY fabric and place it on the end N of the knitting until all sts have been picked up.

2   To knit a section, cast on 28 sts in MY and dec 1 st with 3 trans tool at RT edge until all sts have been dec. With wrong side of work facing, and CY, pick up 1 st at the end of diagonal and K 1 R. Cont picking up 1 st ev R until all sts have been picked up. K 4 R in MY.

3   **Turning**
Cast on 28 sts and K 20 R. Take off onto WY. Place sts back onto machine but with K side facing. Remove WY and K 20 R.

4   To work on every other needle, first check that your machine will select Fair Isle on every other needle; some will not.
Cast on 20 sts over alt N using e-wrap method and 2 ends of MY. K 4 R. Using punchcard for the body of ski sweater (page 76) and CY in 2nd feed, set machine to K Fair Isle. K 24 R. K 4 R str.

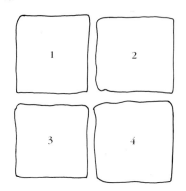

ODD MATERIALS

There are many unconventional materials you can use to make fabrics. This does not just relate to garment design; think of these fabrics as textiles that you can use in other ways, such as for wall hangings or floor coverings.

A nice way of achieving surprise effects is to undo structures which have been made with fibers; they do not necessarily have to be knitted structures. Carpets sometimes unravel to produce interesting yarn substitutes, and some heavy tweeds provide good lengths. Fray them carefully, and remember that they will not have as much stretch as a normal yarn, and will snap more easily. Bits extracted from tweed are effective used for weaving in and you could perhaps use a piece of the tweed in the garment itself.

Ripped fabric knits up well, but you will probably find that you get better results working on every other, or every third needle, or even on a heavier gauge machine, unless you can rip or cut the strips very finely. Here again the unripped fabric could be incorporated into the design. Look for different things to take apart or undo for reknitting.

Leather is a most useful material because, like felt, when it is cut it does not fray, it is quite strong and stretches a little. You can weave it in if the strips are even and fine enough, or thread it through after knitting. It can be used for trims or bindings, and because it is possible to punch holes in it, you can hook it onto the needles and knit it.

Normally you have to take care when washing knitted fabrics but when you reverse the treatment in a controlled way, unusual results can be achieved. When a wool sweater is washed incorrectly, it shrinks and takes on the appearance of felt. This can be used to advantage.

As with all other knitting it is essential to do a few samples to test how they are going to react – for example, you must deal with the shrinkage. When you have a few samples you can either boil them, or put them into the washing machine. It is best to start off with mild treatment so that you can gauge exactly how much heat and time is needed. Remember to measure the swatches before treating them to allow for shrinkage.

You will find that wools are suitable for felting, and interesting effects can be achieved when wool is mixed with a fiber such as cotton that will not shrink. Generally all you have to remember is to use a higher temperature than the wash tag advises and the fabric should felt.

THE SWATCHES

1   Polythene and denim cotton
Denim cotton is used with trash can liners cut into strips across the top of the bag to give circles which are used double. Set the machine to knitweave, TD 7 and set punchcard 1 (page 137). Weave in the polythene. This fabric is soft, and you can even press it with a cool iron over a cloth to bed it in further.

2   Fishing lines
The main yarn is fine variegated line with 2 contrast colors of bulk thread. TD 7, set the machine to knitweave and punchcard 1 (page 137). Weave in with cream CY over 12 sts and gray over next 12 sts, crossing the 2 yarns where they join to form a seam effect.

3   Wire and cotton
This makes an interesting effect; the exposed ends should be twisted together to finish off.
MY = cotton, CY = colored fuse wire
TD 6, cast on 24 sts and K 4 R. *Put LT 18 N to HP. Set machine to hold. Hand feed CY into carr and K 2 R over lst 6 sts only. Put RT 18 N to HP and K 2 R CY over 6 sts at LT end. Set machine to knit and K 2 R MY only.* Rep from * to *.
Put 6 sts at each end to HP. Set machine to hold and K 2 R over center 12 sts in CY. Set machine to knit, K 4 R MY. Rep from ** to **. K 2 R MY. Then rep patt from * to *, then ** to **. K 4 R MY.

4   Rouleau
This is a round cord of knitting. If it is made fine enough, it can be knitted to use up ends of yarn left over.

Gather together odd pieces of yarn of similar thicknesses (maximum 4-ply) and knit them into a continuous rouleau as follows.

Cast on 1-2 sts and K a few rows. Engage the FM button in one direction only. K str. You will notice that the knitting curves back on itself but is secured by the free-move row. On double bed machines, set both carriages to tubular.

Do a few samples to check that the thickness is correct for your type of machine. Test them by putting a piece over the hook of the needle and manually knitting one stitch to see how it will work, then make the necessary adjustments.

When knitting, treat it as you would a normal yarn; try a thicker rouleau on every other needle and double up or tighten the gauge for finer ones.

TD 10. Cast on using e-wrap on every other N. Put N into HP for lst few R. K as normal.

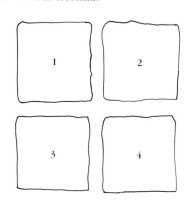

MIXING PATTERNS

Once you have learned and tried the basic techniques, it is important to know how they can be mixed together within one fabric. There are infinite combinations of textures and structures available to the machine knitter, and it is surprisingly simple to develop your own combinations, even if you have little experience in using a machine. For example, gauge can be altered within any fabric to a certain extent, provided that it is not too tight.

It is worth looking at traditional handknitting to see what combinations work best visually when you are mixing patterns. Whatever you decide to experiment with, it is important to make swatches; even if something does not work out as you intended, it may lead to an interesting fabric – so keep all experiments and instructions.

When developing fabric in this way, choose functions on your machine which are compatible, both technically and visually. For example, if you mix lace and Fair Isle (3), use a Fair Isle stitch that enhances the lace – a regular small repeat or an isolated repeat leaving areas free from floats so that you can read the lace pattern. If you use hand selection or a single motif, the Fair Isle and lace are controlled individually which makes the work easier and more versatile. Lace, cable and wale deflection can be mixed (2) to produce a simple fabric.

The cable and stripe combination (1) is a good example of a basic way to mix patterns, experimenting with color and texture. Cables can be mixed with many techniques, including textured stitches such as moss stitch, for example (7).

Isolated weaving and tucking (4) provides an opportunity for a more subtle approach. Definition can be strengthened by using fewer, more highly contrasting colors than I have here.

THE SWATCHES

All fabrics are worked in Rowan Botany Wool, TD 7, 40 R and 36 sts to 10cm (4in). Details given are for the dimensions of swatches.

Yarn color

A = cream, B = gold, C = slate, D = red, E = green, F = black, G = yellow

1   Cables and stripes

The bed is divided into 2 sections for striping (12 sts) and 3 for cabling (6 sts).
Using A, cast on 49 sts. K 3 R. With two 3 trans tools, take LT 3 sts onto LT trans tool and RT 3 sts onto RT trans tool. Put RT 3 sts onto LT 3 empty N and put LT 3 sts onto RT 3 empty N. The cable is complete. Set carr to hold and bring cable section N forward to WP. *Work 2 R in D, working between cable sections. Set carr to knit and work 4 R in A. Work a 3 × 3 cable over 6 sts in cable sections only*. Using col sequence EA, BA, CA, DA, rep from * to *. You may find that the cast on and bound off edges are slightly distorted. This may be lessened by adding a rib or welt and decreasing the gauge on the stripe row. If you like the scalloped effect, you can accentuate it by knitting the stripe rows on a looser gauge, or by cabling more frequently. (See page 40 for details of how to rob yarn for more frequent cables.)

2   Lace, cable and wale deflection

Cast on 50 sts and K 4 R. Cable over center 6 sts. Trans st 12 each side of center to adjacent N to LT and leave empty N in WP. Move 6 edge sts out 1 st and dec 1 st at side edge. Fill empty N with P loop from st to LT. K 2 R. Trans sts 11 and 13 to adjacent N to RT and move out 6 sts as before. K 2 R. Cont cabling over 6 sts ev 4 R and moving out 6 edge sts ev 2 R. The lace panel patt is worked over sts 11, 12 and 13. Cont until R 56. Drop st each side of cable and latch up to make P st.

3   Fair Isle and lace

This is knitted using hand selection over lace and Fair Isle. To hand select Fair Isle, set machine to knit Fair Isle but don't insert punchcard. With A in main feeder, and C in 2nd feeder, any N selected to UWP will K in C and all other sts will K in A. Using A, cast on 40 sts. K 4 R. *Except for center 7 N, trans ev alt st to adjacent N at LT and leave empty N in WP. Push center N to UWP. K 1 R. Bring the 2 N each side of center to UWP. K 1 R.
Except for center 9 N, trans ev alt st not used on last trans R to adjacent N at RT. Push center and next alt N both sides to UWMP. K 1 R.
Cont in this way until 10 R of Fair Isle are worked. Work in reverse until diamond is completed * Rep from * to * twice more. K 4 R.

4   Isolated weaving, tuck and stripe

With A, cast on 42 sts. K 2 R. Using punchcard 1, set machine to K tuck st. Work 1 R. *Lay C, D and E over RT, center and LT 4 N in HP or UWP for pre-selecting machines, or use nylon cord. Work 2 R.* Rep from * to * 11 times more. Now put B into main feeder and work 6 R, still weaving in C, D and E. Rep the block and stripe 2 times more, always weaving in with C, D and E but working horizontal stripe in F.

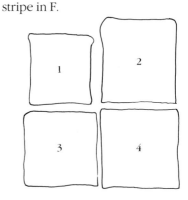

You do not have to be subtle when mixing patterns. Fair Isle can be quite versatile and will mix effectively with other techniques (3, 5, 6, 8, 10). Mixed with holding techniques (5), Fair Isle can be further enhanced by using several different cards and more color changes.

The Fair Isle and wale deflection (6) causes the Fair Isle to distort and would make an attractive neckline or edge detail, or it could be used as part of the overall fabric.

The small Fair Isle repeats and cable (8) illustrate the importance of compatible techniques. The cable reads nicely with the vertical stripe; a more complex Fair Isle would have lost the cables. By applying the holding techniques to this, you could insert wedges or blocks of color, distorting the look further (5).

THE SWATCHES

Yarn color
A = cream, B = gold, C = slate

D = red, E = green, F = black, G = yellow

5 Holding and Fair Isle
Using A, cast on 48 sts. K 4 R. Set machine to knit Fair Isle with the ski sweater border punchcard (page 76). Put CY G in 2nd feeder and K 2 R. *Push 8 N at opposite end to HP on next and ev alt R 4 times. Push 8 N back from HP to WP on next and alt R until all N are in WP.* Change CY to D and K 1 R. Rep from * to * in col sequence E and C. K 4 R.

6 Fair Isle and wale deflection
A 6 trans tool is suggested here, but the fabric can be made with a 1, 2 or 3 trans tool, though it will take longer. N must be realigned for the next patt R for pre-select machines. Here I have pushed back the 2 end N ev R to form a neat edge.
Using A, cast on 54 sts. K 2 R. Using punchcard 1 (page 137), K 1 R. Add C to feeder 2. *With 6 trans tool, take 6 sts to RT of 0 and move them all over

1 st. Rep in the same pos on the LT. Now fill the empty N with the loop formed by the previous R on the N to the LT (of the empty N on the LT) and the N on the RT (of the empty N on the RT). Work 2 rows.*
Rep from * to * until you trans onto the 4th N from the edge, then reverse the process to form a diamond patt.

7 Cable and moss stitch
A ribber was used for this swatch but it could be knitted on a single bed machine using a latch tool.
With A, cast on 56 sts. K 1 R K1 P1 rib. K 1 R st st. *Trans all sts to back bed except for N 25, 18 and 4 each side of center. TD 5 K 4 R. Work cable over 3 sets of 6 sts. K 4 R. Rep cable and trans st 11 each side of center to front bed. K 2 R. Trans st 11 to back bed, then trans sts 10 and 12 to front bed. K 2 R. Cont in this way, cabling ev 4 R and inc trans of sts to and from back bed until only 1 st is left on back bed each side of moss st diamond. Now reverse trans of sts until diamond is completed.* Rep from * to *. K 4 R.

8 Fair Isle and cables
This sample was produced by cabling at random. To do this, use your eye to balance the cable spacing. If you want a regular look, see page 40.
With A, cast on 50 sts. K 2 R. *Using punchcard 1 stopped, add E to feeder 2 and work 6 rows Fair Isle. Cable as for 4 but work at random.* Rep from * to *.

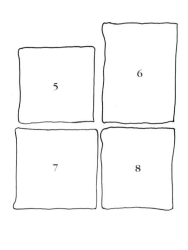

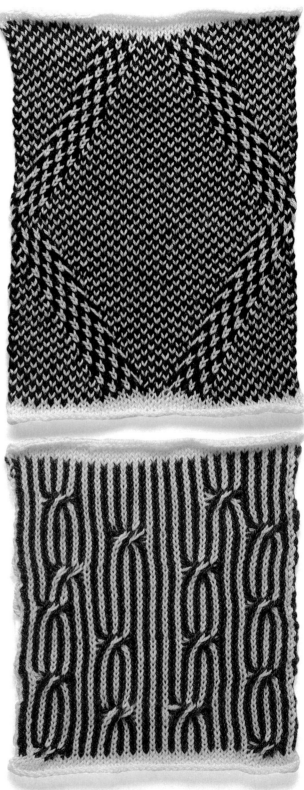

Shape can be affected by changing techniques. Changing from tuck to Fair Isle (11) causes distortion which could be useful for cuffs and neck trims. By mixing techniques you can change the shape of the fabric; for example, tuck stitches hold the fabric out more than stockinette stitch. Going from tuck to Fair Isle and back again (11) makes a difference to the width of the fabric. The frill (12) is made by holding. It could be more decorative still with tiny bits of intarsia, or even a single-motif Fair Isle in the center.

Because isolated weaving is laid over the needles by hand, it is possible to make any image and to create mock intarsia (10). The lace is hand transferred on the stockinette stitch area. This idea could be reversed, using the weaving within the central area.

Intarsia can be mixed with texture as in handknitting; here it is worked with cables (9). Inserting texture into the work by isolating a specific area can be as simple as an intarsia motif in rib or moss stitch.

Punchcards provide endless possibilities for mixing patterns. If you feed in two punchcards together, say a large repeat and a small repeat, the plain areas on the larger repeat will be broken up by the smaller repeat. You can see how this might look by holding the cards together up to the light or laying them together onto a piece of paper and drawing through the holes with a pencil.

THE SWATCHES

Yarn color
A = cream, B = gold, C = slate
D = red, E = green, F = black,
G = yellow

9 Intarsia and cable
Using A cast on 46 sts and K 4 R. Set machine for intarsia and K 4 R. Cable over both sets of 6 sts at edge of knitting and commence intarsia patt over center st with C, with small motifs in B, D, E and C. Cont with intarsia, adding an extra st both sides ev alt R until 15 sts in patt. Start small motifs on R 13 and R 45, *at the same time* cabling ev 4 R over 6 sts at edge until patt is complete. K 4 R.

10 Weaving and lace
If your machine does not pre-select N to UWP, then select by hand. Using A cast on 40 sts and K 4 R. Using punchcard 1 (page 137), set machine to knitweave. Using 2 separate balls of CY C for weaving, lay yarn over all N each side of center N and K 1 R. Lay the yarn over N but leave the center N empty. K 2 R.
Cont in this way, leaving an extra 2 sts empty in center until R 18. Trans center st to adjacent N at LT, K 2 R. Trans 2 n each side of center st to adjacent N at RT. K 2 R.
Cont lace and weaving patt until 5 sts have been trans. Now work lace diamond in reverse and cont weaving until only center st is left empty. K 4 R.

11 Fair Isle and tuck
Using A, cast on 40 sts and K 4 R. Using punchcard 1 (page 137), set machine to K tuck st. K 20 R tuck with A and then 2 R st st. With A in main feeder and C in 2nd yarn feeder, K 14 R Fair Isle. K 2 R st st with A and then 20 R tuck st. K 4 R st st.

12 Frill
Using A, cast on 40 sts and K 4 R. Set machine to hold and push center 10 N to HP. K 4 R and then K 2 R over all sts. Cont rep these 6 R until R 104. K 4 R.

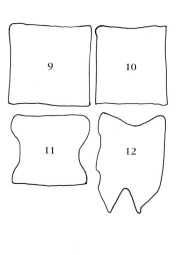

THE COLLECTION

THE COTTON COLLECTION pages 66-75

THE SPORT COLLECTION   pages 76-87

THE CLASSIC COLLECTION pages 88-97

THE COUNTRY COLLECTION pages 98-115

T-SHIRT

The T-shirt is a most popular garment with all age groups. The alternative here has a V neckline with an eyelet and rib detail inset into the V. Eyelets worked along the seams combine with the neckline to give an interesting detail.

This pattern is suitable for knitters with some experience, and can be knitted on all standard gauge machines. Please read through the pattern completely before starting to knit.

SIZES

(Figures for larger sizes are given in square brackets)
To fit 86[91:97:102]cm/34[36:38:40]in chest

Finished measurements

Chest   112[117:122:127]cm/
                 44[46:48:50]in
Length   63[64:65:66]cm/
                 24½[25:25½:26]in
Sleeve length 30cm/12in

MATERIALS

400g/14½oz. Rowan Soft Cotton in true blue Lacy T-shirt in bleached white

GAUGE

MG = 32 sts and 42 R to 10cm (4in) sq measured over st st
TD approx 5
Hems approx 3
Please match gauges accurately before commencing the garment.

PATTERN NOTES

The knit side of the fabric is used as the right side throughout. It is important that the edges of the knitting are perfect to enable a good join.
All stitch transfers are worked with a 7 st trans tool, unless otherwise stated.
To work st trans patt at sides and underarm seams, use 7 st trans tool to pick up sts 2-8 counting in from each edge. Trans outwards, and rehang onto N 1-7, leaving N 8 in WP. For plain T-shirt, fill N 8 with P loop from adjacent N 9. For lacy T-shirt, leave N in WP, but do not fill with P loop. Rep every 4th R.

BACK

Push up 176[184:192:200] N, and using WY cast on. K 16 R in WY.
Change to MY.
TD 3, K 10 R. TD 2, K 5 R. TD 3 K 10 R.
Pick up first R of sts in MY, and hang onto N, making welt.
Reset RC 000. TD 5.
K str to RC 158, working trans patt at both edges every 4th R.

Shape Armhole

Bind off 4 sts beg next 2 R.
Dec 1 st at each end of R, K 3 R, 20 times altogether.
RC 220. 128[136:144:152] sts rem.
K str to RC 248[254:260:266].

Shoulder Shaping

Set carr to hold.**
At side opposite to carr, push 5 N to HP. K 1 R. Push 1 N at same side as carr to HP, and push 5 N to HP at opposite side. K 1 R.
At both sides of work push 1 N to HP. K 1 R. Rep until 8 N are in HP at both sides.**
These 4 R form the shaping sequence. Rep from ** to ** until RC 260[266:272:278].

Back Neck Shaping

Using length of MY, bind off center 36 sts. Work RT side first. Push all N to LT of center to HP.
Using 7 st trans tool, dec 1 st at neck edge every R, at the same time cont shoulder shaping. When 6 neck dec have been worked, set machine to knit back from HP and K 3 R over all N. Change to WY, K 20 R, release from machine.
Rep for second side, reversing shapings.

FRONT

Work as for Back to RC 226[232:238:244].

Front Neck Shaping

Using length of MY, bind off center 8 sts. Divide work placing all N at LT of center into HP. Set carr to hold. Work on RT side only. Using 7 st trans tool, dec 1 st ff every R, 20 times at LT side of work, and cont shaping at RT side for armhole until 20 sts are dec at RT. K str to RC 248[254:260:266].

Shape Shoulders

As for Back from ** to end, omitting Back neck shapings.

Joining Shoulders

Place corresponding Back shoulder sts onto N with wrong sides tog. Unravel WY from back shoulder. TD 10, K 1 R in MY. Bind off using 2 ends MY.
Reset RC to 226[232:238:244]. K LT side reversing all shapings.

NECK BAND

Pick up Front and Back necklines evenly, rehanging work onto machine. 125 N approx, with K side facing you. TD 10, K 1 R. TD 3, K 5 R. TD 2, K 3 R. TD 3, K 5 R.
Pick up first R of band onto corresponding N, and bind off as for shoulders. Join second shoulder as instructions given.

SLEEVES

(Knit two)
Push up 100 N. Cast on, and K welt as for Back. RC 000.
K to RC 50 str.
Bind off 4 sts beg next 2 R. Dec 1 st both ends of work, K 3 R, 20 times altogether. RC 112. 52 sts rem.
Change to WY. K 20 R, release from machine.

MAKING UP

Rehang armhole edge onto machine with K side facing. Hang sleeve onto corresponding N, matching center of cap with shoulder seam. Distribute fullness evenly. Remove WY, bind off as for shoulder seams.

Join side seams in the same way, rehanging onto machine with P sides tog. Bind off using 2 ends of MY. Join sleeve seams in same way. Steam all seams, and give garment final light pressing.

LACY T-SHIRT

K as for previous garment, except for the foll:

Work trans patt as for lace throughout (see Pattern Notes). Make Front neck opening at RC 210[216:222:228]. Using 6 trans tool, trans 6 sts either side of center N, ff, 1 N towards center. Leave empty N in work. K 2 R.

Rep these instructions moving out 1 N each time, forming diagonal row of holes, until there are 9 holes on each side.

To make ribbed V inset, leave center N. Take alt N on either side and drop sts from N 1 at a time. Let st run down to R above hole. Use latch

tool to pick up, and latch up to top on side facing you. This will form a 1 × 1 rib in the section at the point of the V.

K 2 R, bind off center 19 sts.

Shape Front Neck

Push all N at LT to HP. Dec 1 st using 7 st trans tool, K 6 R, 10 times altogether. When RC reads 248[254:260:266], start shoulder shaping as for Back. Put onto WY. Rep for second side reversing shapings.

Shape Back Neck

Work as for the Back of T-shirt except binding off 28 sts instead of 36 sts at center Back.

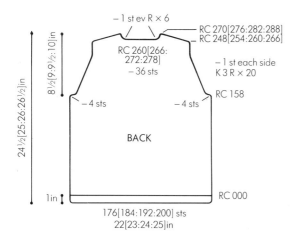

8½[9:9½:10]in

24½[25:26:26½]in

1in

− 1 st ev R × 6

RC 270[276:282:288]
RC 248[254:260:266]

RC 260[266:
272:278]
− 36 sts

− 1 st each side
K 3 R × 20

RC 158

− 4 sts   − 4 sts

BACK

RC 000

176[184:192:200] sts
22[23:24:25]in

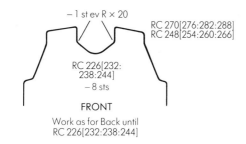

− 1 st ev R × 20

RC 270[276:282:288]
RC 248[254:260:266]

RC 226[232:
238:244]
− 8 sts

FRONT

Work as for Back until
RC 226[232:238:244]

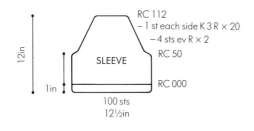

12in

1in

RC 112
− 1 st each side K 3 R × 20
− 4 sts ev R × 2
RC 50

SLEEVE

RC 000

100 sts
12½in

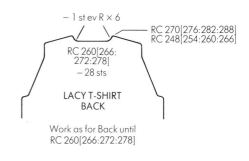

− 1 st ev R × 6

RC 270[276:282:288]
RC 248[254:260:266]

RC 260[266:
272:278]
− 28 sts

LACY T-SHIRT
BACK

Work as for Back until
RC 260[266:272:278]

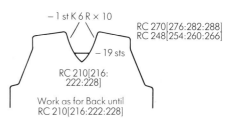

− 1 st K 6 R × 10

RC 270[276:282:288]
RC 248[254:260:266]

− 19 sts

RC 210[216:
222:228]

Work as for Back until
RC 210[216:222:228]

LACY T-SHIRT
FRONT

DENIM SKIRT

This skirt is knitted in cotton which shrinks and fades like denim. The short pleated variation is knitted sideways.

LONG SKIRT

This pattern is suitable for all standard gauge machines, and for knitters with some experience.

SIZES

(Figures for larger sizes are given in square brackets)
To fit 86[91:97:102]cm/34[36:38:40]in hip

Finished measurements after shrinking and pressing

Waist	63[68:73:78]cm/ 25[27:29:31]in
Length	74cm/29in

MATERIALS

500g/18oz Rowan Indigo Dyed Cotton in 4-ply
1 × 20cm (8in) lightweight zipper
1 small (1½cm/¾in) button
Length of 2cm (¾in) waistband elastic to fit

GAUGE

MG = 32 sts and 50 R to 10cm (4in) sq measured after washing, shrinking and pressing.
TD approx 6 o.
It is essential to wash this swatch to obtain an accurate reading. Please match gauge accurately before commencing garment.

PATTERN NOTES

Knit side of fabric is used as the right side throughout. This long skirt is knitted from hem to waist. All shapings are worked using 7 trans tool unless otherwise stated. Wash, shrink and press garment after assembling sections to obtain required finish.

BACK PANELS

(Knit 2, reversing side seam shaping)
Push up 120[124:128:132] N to WP.
Using WY, cast on and K 20 R at MG.
Using MY, K 1 R. Set TD 5 o, K 7 R. TD 10, K 1 R. TD to 6o, K 7 R. Hook up welt, remove WY. K 1 R. Reset RC 000. Work edge detail as foll:
Dec 1 st both ends using 7 trans tool. Push empty edge N to UWP to pick up on next R. Rep from * to * every 4th R.
At the same time, at RC 10, commence godet shaping as foll: Starting at center of work, move all sts in 1 N on each side of 0. Center 2 N now carry 2 sts each. Push empty N at each edge to NWP. Work this dec every 10 R, 12 times altogether. RC 120. 96[100:104:108] sts rem.
Cont forming edge detail on both sides every 4 R, and dec 1 st both ends at RC 144, 168, 192, 216, 240, by not returning emptied N to UWP. K str to RC 252.

Side Seam Shaping

Dec 1 st at side seam edge in same manner as before on every 16th R (at RC 252:268:284:300:316:332:348). Dec 1 st at side edge every 2 R, 4 times altogether. RC 356. K str on this edge to RC 364.
At the same time at RC 324, commence waist dart shaping as foll: Starting at center 2 N each have 2 inwards 1 N (center 2 N each have 2 sts), every 10 R, 5 times altogether (at RC 324:334:344:354:364). Change to WY, K 20 R, remove from machine.

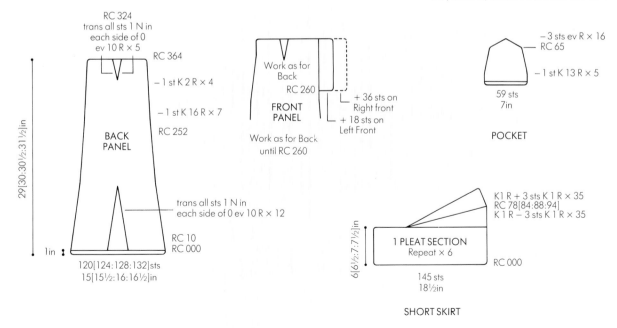

RC 324
trans all sts 1 N in each side of 0 ev 10 R × 5
RC 364
−1 st K 2 R × 4
−1 st K 16 R × 7
BACK PANEL
RC 252
29[30:30½:31½]in
trans all sts 1 N in each side of 0 ev 10 R × 12
RC 10
RC 000
1in
120[124:128:132]sts
15[15½:16:16½]in

Work as for Back
RC 260
FRONT PANEL
Work as for Back until RC 260
+ 36 sts on Right front
+ 18 sts on Left Front

−3 sts ev R × 16
RC 65
−1 st K 13 R × 5
59 sts
7in
POCKET

K 1 R + 3 sts K 1 R × 35
RC 78[84:88:94]
K 1 R − 3 sts K 1 R × 35
6[6½:7:7½]in
1 PLEAT SECTION
Repeat × 6
RC 000
145 sts
18½in
SHORT SKIRT

RIGHT FRONT PANEL

Work as for Back to RC 260. Cast on 18 sts at center front by e-wrap method. K 2 R. Trans st 10 at RT side to adjacent N. Push N 10 to NWP. Work to end as for Back panel, but bring up N 10 to WP at RC 364. Remove on WY as Back panel.

LEFT FRONT PANEL

Work as for Right front panel, but e-wrap cast on 36 sts at center front. Trans st 18 to adjacent N, push N 18 to NWP.
K to RC 362 following Back panel patt. Bring N 18 to WP. K 2 R. Change to WY. K 20 R, remove from machine.

POCKETS

(Knit two)
Push up 59 N. Using WY, cast on and K 20 R. Change to MY. TD 6○ K 1 R. TD 5○ K 7 R. TD 10 K 1 R. TD 6○, K 7 rows. Hook up welt. Unravel WY. RC 000. TD 6○.
K 13 R. Dec 1 st both ends ff, using 7 trans tool, 5 times altogether (on R 13:26:39:52:65). 49 sts rem.
Bind off 3 sts beg every R until 1 st rem . Bind off.

MAKING UP

Hang side of Back panel on N, picking up larger loops down side, with K side facing. Hang side of Front panel onto same N in the same way with P side facing you.
K 1 row across by hand, then bind off around gate pegs.
Rep with second Front and Back.

WAISTBAND

Rehang sts from RT half of skirt onto N, to ladder st in placket. K side facing, placing 2 sts onto every 10th N, 6 times, giving 2 panels of 60 sts (120[128:136:144] N in WP in all). Fold placket in half, and hang sts on corresponding N. Unravel WY.
K 4 R MG. * Set carr to hold and push all N to HP except 5 N at center Front. K 6 R over these sts. Push these N to HP and work 6 R over all other N.* K 4 over all N MG, K 1 R TD 10, K 4 R

MG. Work from * to * once more and then K 4 MG over all N. Hook up sts from first, R K 1 R MG and bind off around gate pegs.
K LT side of waistband in the same way but omitting buttonhole, taking into account the extra 10 sts on the placket.
Join center Front and center Back seams in the same way as the side seams and sew button onto waistband. Sew on pockets on back as on denim jeans. Insert the zipper.

SHORT SKIRT

This pattern is suitable for knitters with some experience, and all double bed or standard gauge machines with ribber fitted. The garment may be knitted on single bed machines, and the waistband made by the hand tool method of ribbing. Read through the pattern completely before starting to knit.

SIZES

(Figures for larger sizes are given in square brackets)
To fit 86[91:97:102]cm/34[36:38:40]in hip

Finished measurements after shrinking and pressing
Waist   63[68:73:78]cm/
           25[27:29:31]in
Length   47cm/18.5in

MATERIALS

500g/18oz Rowan Indigo Dyed Cotton in 4-ply.
Length of 2cm (¾in) waistband elastic to fit

GAUGE

MG = 32 sts and 50 R to 10cm (4in) sq
TD approx 6 ○ after washing
Please match gauges accurately before commencing the garment.

PATTERN NOTES

Knit side of the fabric is used as the right side throughout. Wash, shrink and press garment after assembling sections to obtain required finish.

Tumble dry garment if possible to aid shrinkage. All shaping is worked using holding techniques (page 34). This is a sideways-knit garment.
To avoid a hole in the work when shaping in hold, wrap yarn *under* last N in HP nearest carr, and leave over all rem HP N, before knitting next R.

SKIRT

Push up 145 N, and using WY, cast on. K 20 R in WY. RC 000. Change to MY. Set carr to knit and MT.
Carr at LT. ** K 78[84:88:94] R str.

Make Pleat
Carr at LT.
At RT of bed, push 40 N to HP. Set carr to knit with N in HP.
TD 8. K 1 R. TD 6. K 1 R. Carr at LT. Push up 3 N to HP in center, K 1 R, 35 times, ensuring end N is wrapped every time. (See Pattern Notes.)
TD 8. Return all N to WP except 40 at RT, K 1 R. TD 6 K 1 R. Carr at LT. TD 6. Push all but edge 3 N to HP K 2 R. Cont pushing 3 N to WP every 2 R until 104 N are in WP. TD 8, K 1 R. TD 6. Carr at LT **. Rep from ** to ** 5 more times, making a total of 6 pleats in all. The skirt will commence with a section of str knitting and end with a pleat. At completion of last pleat, change to WY, K 20 R. Release from machine.

WAISTBAND

Push up 112[120:128:136] N on both beds, and arrange for 2 × 1 welt. Using MY, cast on and K 66 R at TD 2 to 3. Trans all sts to back bed. Rehang exactly half skirt width onto these N, with wrong side of skirt facing you. K 1 R and bind off. Rep for other half of skirt.

MAKING UP

Graft seam up skirt. Join waistband seams. Turn waistband to inside and catch down, inserting length of elastic to fit.
Wash, shrink and tumble dry. Press, folding pleats of skirt at loose rows to form inverted pleats.

BASIC SHIRT

The shirt has a yoke effect produced by wale deflection on either side of the placket. It resembles a man's dress shirt – the back is longer than the front – and though knitted up here in Rowan's Soft Cotton, it would look good in silk or wool for a more formal garment. The basic structure could be given more shape with the addition of shoulder pads.

The short-sleeved alternative has been worked in a one-row striped fabric with the reverse side showing.

This pattern is suitable for knitters with some experience, and can be knitted on all standard gauge machines. Please read through the pattern completely before starting to knit.

SIZES

(Figures for larger sizes are given in square brackets)
To fit 86[91:97:102]cm/34[36:38:40]in chest

Finished measurements

Chest   112[117:122:127]cm/
                44[46:48:50]in
Back length   71.5[72.5:74:75]cm/
                28[28½:29:29½]in
Front length   64[65.5:67:68.5]cm/
                25[25½:26:26½]in
Sleeve length   51cm/20in
Short sleeve   26.5cm/10½in
length

MATERIALS

400g/14½oz Rowan Soft Cotton in eau de nil
4 shirt buttons
For striped version:
150g/5½oz Rowan Soft Cotton in Turkish plum (MY) and ecru (CY)

GAUGE

MG = 32 sts and 44 R to 10cm (4in) sq
TD approx 5 for main fabric
TD approx 3 and 2 for welts
Please match gauges accurately before commencing the garment.

PATTERN NOTES

Knit side of the fabric is used as the right side. All transfers are worked with a 7 trans tool, unless otherwise stated. It is important that the edges of the work are perfect to enable a good graft when making up.
Edge Stitch Transfer Pattern (or wale deflection) is worked on every 4th R, in the following way. Using 7 st trans tool, pick up sts 2–8 at edge. Trans outwards, and rehang onto N 1–7. Fill empty N 8 with P loop from N 9. Rep at opposite side.
Center Front Transfer Pattern is worked by moving sts 11–34 on both sides of center out to N 12–35. Fill empty N 11 with P loop from N 10. Rep every 4th R.

BACK

Push up 176[184:192:200] N, and using WY, cast on, K 20 R in WY. Change to MY.
TD 3, K 10 R. TD 2, K 5 R. TD 3, K 10 R. Pick up first row of sts. TD 5, RC 000, K 2 R, unravel WY.
Cont to K str to RC 186[190:196:200], working st trans patt at edges. (See Pattern Notes.)

Armhole Shaping

Bind off 8 sts beg next 2 R.
K 10 R, dec 1 st each end, 10 times altogether.
Cont to K str and commence Back neck shaping at RC 292[296:302:306]. Using a length of MY, bind off center 28 sts. Push all N to LT of center to HP. Set carr to hold.
Dec 1 st at neck edge every R, 6 times. 50[54:58:62] sts rem.
Change to WY. K 20 R, remove from machine. Rep shaping on LT side.

FRONT

Push up 176[184:192:200] N, and follow instructions for Back to RC 90[94:98:102]. Commence Center Trans Patt (see Pattern Notes), and cont working side trans patt to RC 120[126:132:138].

Shape Front Opening

Using length of MY, bind off center 8 sts. Push all N at RT of center to HP. Set carr to hold. Using WY, K 20 R. Release from machine. Work on RT side, using MY, and cont trans patt at edge and center. K str to RC 154[160:166:172].

Shape Armhole

Bind off 8 sts at armhole edge, K 2 R. K 10 R, dec 1 st at armhole edge, 10 times altogether. At the same time at RC 219 [223:229:233], bind off 5 sts at neck edge, K 2 R.
** Dec 1 st, K 2 R, 11 times altogether. Work str until armhole dec are complete. K to RC 266[272: 278:284].
Rehang back shoulder on same N, P sides tog. Unravel WY. Bind off both Front and Back tog.
Rehang LT side of front onto N. Unravel WY, and K reversing all shapings. Bind off Back and Front tog.

COLLAR

Rehang neckline onto machine over approx 116 N (126 for short-sleeved shirt), with K side of garment facing you. *K 2 R.
Inc 1 st both ends, every 4th R, 6 times. K 2 R. RC 28. Bind off.

Collar Binding

With K side of collar facing you, rehang collar edge onto N.
Using MY, e-wrap cast on (see page 120) an additional 20 N at each side. K 2 R in MY. Bind off. This will form a roll edge which will press flat.*

SLEEVES

Push up 60 N, and K welt as for Back and Front. RC 000.
Using 7 trans tool, inc 1 st both ends every 4th R, 46 times. RC 184. 152 sts rem. K str to RC 209.
Change to WY, K 20 R, release from machine.

BANDS

Button Band

With K side facing, pick up 68 sts LT side of front opening, and rehang onto N. With MY, TD 3, K 8 R. TD 2, K 5 R. TD 3, K 8 R. Pick up first row onto N to make welt, bind off.

Buttonhole Band

Work as for button band, picking up RT side of opening. TD 3, K 5 R. Counting from upper edge of opening, make buttonholes over N 7 and 8, 25 and 26, 43 and 44, 61 and 62, in the foll way:

Move sts from N outwards to adjacent N. Leave N in WP. K 1 R. Using loop of yarn on N, e-wrap empty N. TD 3, K 2 R. TD 2, K 5 R. TD 3, K 3 R. Rep buttonholes. TD 3, K 5 R. Pick up first R onto N to make welt. Bind off.

MAKING UP

With P side facing, rehang armhole edge onto N. Do not hang first 8 sts at each end as these will form part of the underarm seam.

With K side facing, and matching center to shoulder seam, rehang sleeve onto N, distributing extra sts evenly over the N. Unravel WY. Bind off both parts together. Pick up the 8 sts at each end onto N. Hang 8 loops from side sleeve onto N. Bind off. Rep for second sleeve.

Hang Back and Front side edges onto N with P sides tog. Bind off. Hang sleeve edges onto N, bind off. Rep for opposite side.

Steam and press, paying particular attention to seams.

STRIPED SHORT-SLEEVED SHIRT

To knit the 1 R striped fabric, work as foll:

K 1 R to RT using MY, K 1 R to LT using CY. Remove CY. Set carr to non knit, pass carr to RT, re-thread MY, K 1 R to LT.

Remove MY, thread CY, K 1 R to RT, and so on, K 1 R in each col.

To knit garment without welts as in the photograph, e-wrap cast on, K 5 R, then follow patt from instructions to turn up welt.

BACK

K as for basic pattern to RC 165[170: 170:175]. Bind off 8 sts beg next 2 R. Dec 1 st each end, K 2 R, 11 times. Foll main patt for neck shaping.

FRONT

Work as for Back to RC 215[220:225: 230]. Working on center 18 sts only, release alt sts 1 at a time, and allow them to run down work 12 R. Pick up with latch tool, and hook up on P side. This will form a 1 × 1 ribbed section in work. Bind off center 8 sts. Follow main patt from **.

COLLAR

Push up 126 N and e-wrap cast on.
Foll main patt from * to *. Hand sew
to neck opening.

SLEEVES

E-wrap cast on by hand over 106 N.
Inc 1 st each end every 4th R, 23
times. RC 92, 152 sts rem. K 25 R str.
Change to WY, K 20 R. Release from
machine.

MAKING UP

Follow main garment patt.

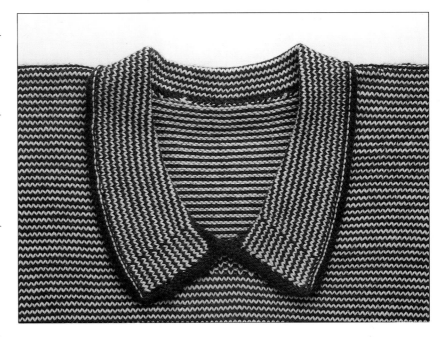

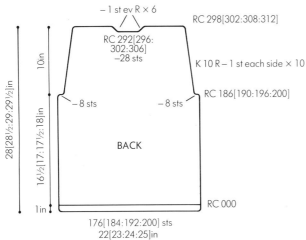

−1 st ev R × 6
RC 298[302:308:312]
RC 292[296:302:306]
−28 sts
K 10 R − 1 st each side × 10
RC 186[190:196:200]
−8 sts   −8 sts

BACK

10in
16½[17:17½:18]in
28[28½:29:29½]in
1in
RC 000

176[184:192:200] sts
22[23:24:25]in

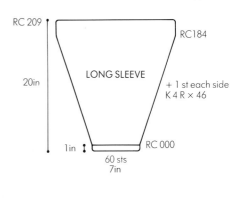

RC 209
RC184

LONG SLEEVE

20in
+ 1 st each side
K 4 R × 46

1in
60 sts
7in
RC 000

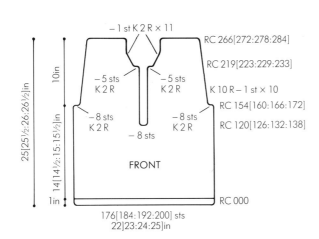

−1 st K 2 R × 11
RC 266[272:278:284]
RC 219[223:229:233]
−5 sts
K 2 R   −5 sts
K 2 R
K 10 R − 1 st × 10
RC 154[160:166:172]
−8 sts
K 2 R   −8 sts
K 2 R
RC 120[126:132:138]
−8 sts

FRONT

10in
14[14½:15:15½]in
25[25½:26:26½]in
1in
RC 000

176[184:192:200] sts
22[23:24:25]in

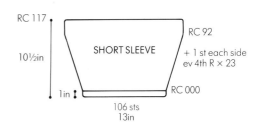

RC 117
RC 92

SHORT SLEEVE

10½in
+ 1 st each side
ev 4th R × 23

1in
106 sts
13in
RC 000

RC 28
+ 1 st each end
ev 4th R × 6
COLLAR
2in
126 sts
15in
RC 2

SKI SWEATER

The Fair Isle fabric and the shape of this ski sweater suggests a 'fifties style of sweater. The 24-stitch repeat of the Fair Isle is built up using traditional motifs mixed with patterns from Islamic carpets. The trim fabric on the border has been knitted sideways and this works well within the normal limitations of a domestic single bed knitting machine.

The nature of the yarn and the small repeat mean that floats across the back of the work build up to produce a warm fabric, ideal for winter weather.

This pattern is suitable for all knitters, and for single bed punch-card machines. For electronic machine owners, copy the punch-card pattern onto the electronic sheet for your machine. Please read through the pattern completely before starting to knit.

SIZES

(Figures for larger size are given in square brackets)
To fit up to 97[106]cm/38[42]in chest

Finished measurements

Chest	114[120]cm/45[47]in
Length	71cm/28in
Sleeve length	49cm/20in

MATERIALS

300g/11oz Rowan Botany Wool in black (MY)
350g/12½oz Rowan Botany Wool in cream (CY)

GAUGE

MG = 34 sts and 36 R to 10cm (4in) sq
TD approx 6 to 7
Please match gauge accurately before commencing garment.

PATTERN NOTES

The knit side of the single bed Fair Isle fabric is used as the right side throughout. MY is in the main yarn feed, and CY in the second feed throughout. All inc and dec are worked at the edge of the fabric using single transfer tool. Knit back of garment with card in the machine right way round. Reverse the card to knit the front, so that the pattern will match on the shoulders. Knit 1 extra row in MY st st at all shoulders before removing from machine.

BACK

Push up 192[200] N and using MY make an e-wrap cast on.
With MY in main yarn feed, and CY in second yarn feed, set to K single-bed Fair Isle. Set to MG. RC 000.
Select R 47 on body punchcard.
K str to RC 118.
Bind off 12 st at beg next 2 R.
K str to RC 196.

Back Neck Shaping
Using odd length of MY, bind off center 32 sts. Push all rem N to LT of center to HP, and set carr to knit RT side only first. *Note number on punchcard.*
At neck edge, dec 1 st, K 3 R, 4 times altogether. RC 208.
K 1 R in st st in MY only. Change to WY, K 20 R, release from machine.
Turn punchcard onto number noted. Return N to WP, and K second side, reversing shapings.

FRONT

Use card reversed for this garment part.
Cast on and work as for Back to RC 170.

Front Neck Shaping
Note number on punchcard.
Using an odd length of MY, bind off center 26 sts. Place all N to LT of center into HP. Work on RT side only first.
At neck edge, dec 1 st, K 5 R, 7 times altogether. K 1 row st st in MY. RC 208.
Change to WY, K 20 R, release from machine.

Return card to marked pos and set carr for single-bed Fair Isle. Reset RC to 172. Rep reversing shapings for opposite side.
Rehang back and front LT shoulder onto machine, with wrong sides together. Remove WY. Using MY, bind off together.

NECK TRIM

Push up 97 N, leaving out center N. Using WY cast on, K 10 R st st. Change to MY in main feed, and CY in feed 2. Insert trim punchcard and select R 1. RC 000.
K str in single-bed Fair Isle to RC 180. Change to WY and set carr to knit. K 10 R.

Neck Join
Rehang whole neck edge onto machine with purl side facing you. Rehang first edge of neck trim onto same N, with purl side facing you. Remove WY. Rehang second edge of trim on same N, doubling trim in half. Remove WY. K 1 R st st with MY. Bind off around gate pegs.
Rehang Back and Front RT shoulder onto machine with wrong sides together. Remove WY. Using MY bind off together.

SLEEVE

(Knit two alike)
Push up 94 N. Using MY cast on using e-wrap method. Insert body punchcard and set to knit single-bed Fair Isle. RC 000.
Inc 1 st at both ends of the next 12 R, then inc 1 st at both ends of the next and ev foll 6th R until 160 sts rem. K to RC 146. Bind off.

SLEEVE TRIM

(Knit two alike)
Push up 56 N. *Using WY cast on. MT. K 10 R st st.
RC 000. Insert trim punchcard into machine. Set carr to single-bed Fair Isle. MG. Set to K patt on N at RT side only, and MY only st st on rem N at LT.

(Single Motif Setting).*
K 104 R in patt. Bind off.

BODY TRIM

(Knit two alike)
Push up 86 N. Cast on as for sleeve trims, foll instructions from * to *. K 190 R str. Bind off.

MAKING UP

Graft cuff onto sleeve. Fold in half with plain st st section to inside. Stitch into place.
Graft body trims to lower ends of body sections, easing to fit. Fold plain section to inside. Catch down. Rehang sides of Back and Front onto machine, taking large loops, purl sides together. K 1 R st st in MY. Bind off around gate pegs. Rep for opposite side.
Rehang sleeve onto machine taking large loops, purl sides together. K 1 R st st in MY. Bind off. Rep for other sleeve.
Graft neck trim seam together.
Give final light steaming and pressing.

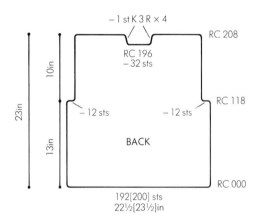

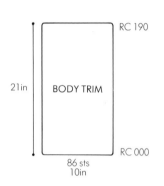

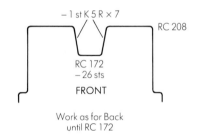

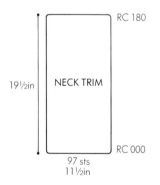

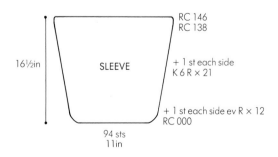

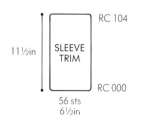

BODY PUNCHCARD: 24-st repeat

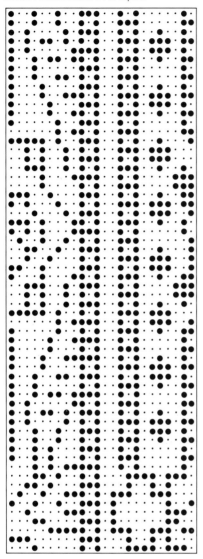

40-st repeat

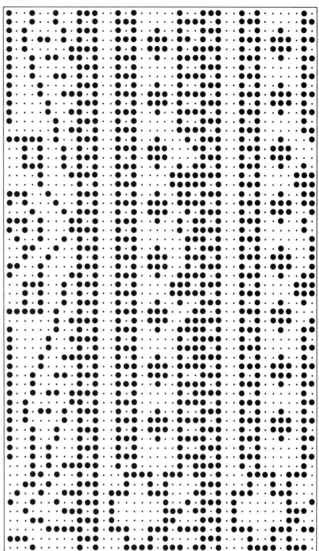

TRIM PUNCHCARD: 24-st repeat

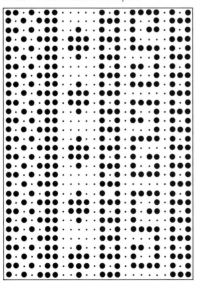

40-st repeat

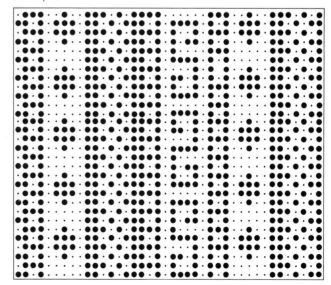

SLACKS

This style is casual and loose fitting with bind-off chains down the creases to give the leg a good shape. The basic fabric is a slip stitch, which produces a float on the reverse side. This makes a thicker and more stable fabric which will keep its shape and will not stretch and bag at the knees and seat. To make sizing and fit easier to calculate, there is an elasticized waist and measurements are given for the crotch depth.

This pattern is suitable for knitters with some experience, and may be knitted on all standard gauge machines. Please read through the pattern completely before starting to knit.

SIZES

(Figures for larger sizes are given in square brackets)
To fit 61[66:71]cm/24[26:28]in waist

Finished measurements

Waist	81[86.5:91.5]cm/32[34:36]in
Hip	99[104:109]cm/39[41:43]in
Length	110[111:111.5]cm/ 43[43½:43½]in
Cuff	20cm/8in

MATERIALS

700g/25oz Rowan Botany Wool in cream
2 × 15cm (6in) lightweight zippers

GAUGE

MG = 40 sts and 64 R to 10cm (4in) sq
TD approx 7 for main fabric
Please match gauges accurately before commencing garment.

PATTERN NOTES

Knit side of the fabric is used as the right side throughout. Main parts of the garment are knitted in a slip stitch using punchcard 1 (page 137). All increases and decreases are worked on edge stitches, unless stated otherwise within the pattern. Center seams of legs have stitched transfer pattern worked as foll:

Using 6 trans tool, move edge sts 1 N inwards. Push emptied edge N to HP. Rep every 4th R.
*** marks pos where garment may be lengthened if required. Knit 16 extra R for every 2.5cm (1in) in length.
The pockets can be cut out of a fabric, such as cotton jersey, if you prefer.

FRONT

Side Front Panel

(Knit 2 reversing shapings)
Push up 36[40:44] N, and using MY make hand cast on. Insert punchcard and set to R 1. Set carr to slip stitch. RC 000.
Work 6 trans patt on RT side of work (what will be center seam).
Inc 1 st at LT edge, K 16 R, 12 times. K 6 R str. RC 198***.
Cont trans patt at RT edge throughout. Inc 1 st at LT edge, K 19 R, 10 times. K 82 R str. RC 470.
At LT side, dec 1 st every 7th R 14 times using 6 trans tool. RC 568. K 0[5:10] R str.
Change to WY and K several R. Remove from machine.

Center Front Panel

(Knit 2 reversing shapings)
Push up 36[40:44] N, and make hand cast on using MY. Set to knit slip patt. Work 6 trans patt on LT.
Inc 1 st at RT edge every 16th R 12 times. K 6 R str. RC 198*** K 8 R str. RC 206.
At the RT edge, inc 1 st every 17th R 8 times. RC 342.
At RT edge, inc 1 st every 6th R 9 times. RC 396.

Shape crotch

At RT edge, dec 2 sts, K 2 R, 6 times. RC 408.
At RT edge, dec 1 st, K 2 R, 7 times. RC 422.
K 146[151:156] R str. RC 568[573:578].
Change to WY and K several R.
Release from machine.

BACK

Side back panel

(Knit 2 reversing shapings)
Push up 42[48:54] N, and cast on by hand using MY. Set to knit slip patt. Trans patt worked on RT edge throughout.
At LT edge, inc 1 st every 15th R 13 times. K 3 R str. RC 198***.
Inc 1 st every 14th R 13 times. RC 380. K 88 R str.
At LT edge, using 6 trans tool, dec 1 st every 6th R 16 times. RC 564.

Waist shaping

At LT edge place 13 N to HP. Set carr to hold. K 4 R.
Rep from * to * 4 times until all N are in HP.
Push N back to WP, and K 0[5:10] R str. Change to WY and K several R. Release from machine.

Center back panel

(Knit 2 reversing shapings)
Push up 42[48:54] N and cast on by hand in MY. Set to knit slip patt. Trans patt worked on LT edge throughout.
At RT edge, inc 1 st every 11th R 18 times. RC 198***.
At RT edge, inc 1 st every 21 R 5 times. K 3 R str. RC 306.
K 20 R str.
At RT edge, inc 1 st every 2nd R 30 times. RC 386.

Crotch shaping

At RT edge, bind off 4 sts every R 3 times. K 1 R.
At RT edge, bind off 2 sts every other R 4 times. At RT edge, dec 1 st every R 14 times. RC 412.
At RT edge, dec 1 st every 4th R 40 times. K str to RC 576.
At RT edge, push 5 N to HP. Set carr to hold, and K 2 R. Rep until all N are in HP.
K 0[5:10] R. RC 578[583:588].
Change to WY and K several R. Release from machine.

Bottom cuff

After joining garment parts Side Front and Center Front at trans patt edge, join Side Back and Center Back at trans patt edge (see below in Making up). Seam the 2 resulting sections down the outside edge of the slacks leg. Push up 128 N to WP. Rehang bottom edge of leg onto N. K 94 R in st st at MG. Bind off on machine.

POCKETS

(Knit 2 as patt and 2 reversing shapings)
Push up 30 N using MY hand cast on. RC 000. Knit in st st at MG.
Inc 1 st at RT side every 4 R, and 1 st at LT side every 8 R. K to RC 72. Inc 1 st both ends every R to RC 112. Push 15 N at RT to HP. Set carr to hold, K 2 R, 4 times altogether. Set carr to knit. K 1 R. Bind off.

MAKING UP

Block and press all parts to size. Hang one Side Front and one Center Front onto N of machine with wrong sides facing. K 1 R. Bind off around gate pegs. Rep for other side. Use same method for joining Side Back and Center Backs, leaving a 15cm (8in) opening each side for zippers.

WAISTBAND

With RT side facing, rehang joined Fronts onto machine. Unravel WY. Using MY and st st at TD 7, K 14 R str. K 1 R TD 9, then 14 R TD 7. Hook up first R, K 1 R and bind off around gate pegs. Knit back waistband in the same way.
Hand sew or link up front and back crotch seams with RT sides facing. Sew zippers to top of both outside seams. Join edges of the pockets together leaving one long sloping edge open to sew over zipper opening. Inset waistband elastic. Give final light pressing.

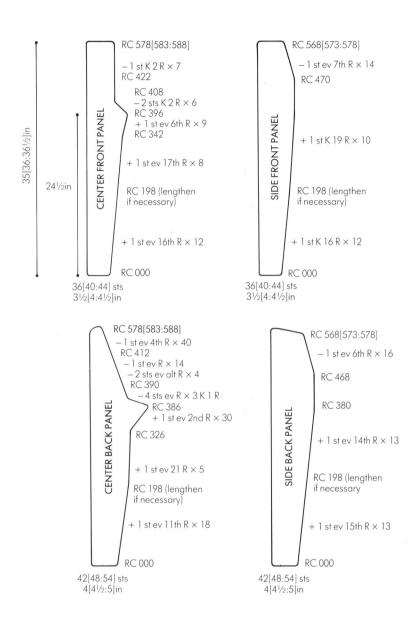

CENTER FRONT PANEL
35[36:36½]in
24½in
RC 578[583:588]
− 1 st K 2 R × 7
RC 422
RC 408
− 2 sts K 2 R × 6
RC 396
+ 1 st ev 6th R × 9
RC 342
+ 1 st ev 17th R × 8
RC 198 (lengthen if necessary)
+ 1 st ev 16th R × 12
RC 000
36[40:44] sts
3½[4:4½]in

SIDE FRONT PANEL
RC 568[573:578]
− 1 st ev 7th R × 14
RC 470
+ 1 st K 19 R × 10
RC 198 (lengthen if necessary)
+ 1 st K 16 R × 12
RC 000
36[40:44] sts
3½[4:4½]in

CENTER BACK PANEL
RC 578[583:588]
− 1 st ev 4th R × 40
RC 412
− 1 st ev R × 14
− 2 sts ev alt R × 4
RC 390
− 4 sts ev R × 3 K 1 R
RC 386
+ 1 st ev 2nd R × 30
RC 326
+ 1 st ev 21 R × 5
RC 198 (lengthen if necessary)
+ 1 st ev 11th R × 18
RC 000
42[48:54] sts
4[4½:5]in

SIDE BACK PANEL
RC 568[573:578]
− 1 st ev 6th R × 16
RC 468
RC 380
+ 1 st ev 14th R × 13
RC 198 (lengthen if necessary
+ 1 st ev 15th R × 13
RC 000
42[48:54] sts
4[4½:5]in

WRAP

This versatile garment is a one-size large rectangle with an opening down the center front. The interest is in the fabric – a plaid pattern with connotations of the Scottish Highlands seemed an obvious choice. It would also be effective knitted plain with detail at the seams.

This pattern is suitable for knitters with a little experience of knitweave techniques, and is suitable for all machines with a knitweave facility, single or double bed.

SIZES

This is a one-size garment to fit up to a 106cm/42in chest

Finished measurements

Length worn	96cm/38in approx
flat	191/75in
Full width	117cm/46in
Front opening	102cm/40in

MATERIALS

1400g/49½oz Rowan Light Tweed in gray (209) (MY)
350g/12½oz Rowan Botany Wool in each of the following: black, pale yellow
50g/2oz Rowan Botany Wool in each of the following: gold, slate, red, green.

GAUGE

MG = 28 sts and 48 R to 10cm (4in) sq
TD approx 5 for main fabric and welts

PATTERN NOTES

The purl side of the fabric is used as the right side throughout. When using more than one color in knitweave, it is easier to feed yarns by hand into the machine from balls or cones on the floor in front of the machine, rather than use the tension antennae or mast to carry yarns.

The garment is knitted in two panels and seamed together on completion. The plaid pattern is formed by setting your machine to knitweave, and hand laying the weaving yarn over selected needles/areas. Mark the needle-bed on the machine to correspond with chart provided to avoid counting needles every row. Use colored adhesive tape to mark the bed on machines with a plastic number strip (e.g. Brother), or mark with crayon for metal bed machines (e.g. Superba).

Mark out each area according to the chart. Numbers along the bottom of the chart represent needles/stitches, and numbers running vertically represent rows of knitting.

You may use different color tapes or crayons for different areas to make knitting even easier.

When knitweaving in small areas of pattern like this, the weaving yarn

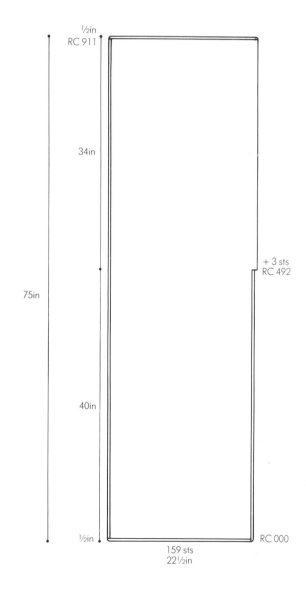

is hand laid over those needles forming the area of color only, rather in the same way as laying yarns for intarsia knitting. Where colors of weaving yarn join, cross yarns in the same way as for intarsia to make an even edge.

As the pattern of the weave is 1 × 1 using punchcard 1 (page 137), note that the number of needles the weaving yarn will be laid over will be different for alternate rows (e.g. 9 in one row, 8 in the next, and so on). Be sure to follow your needle-bed markers to obtain straight vertical lines in the pattern. Note that the large stripes on the chart have the MY changed as well as the contrast.

LEFT PANEL

Push up 159 N and using WY, cast on and K a few R. Change to MY and K 6 R st st. TD 10 K 1 R. TD 5 K 6 R. Turn up welt in the foll way:
Pick up first row in MY, and rehang onto N, Remove WY.
RC 000. Insert punchcard 1 and set machine to knitweave. Commencing at the bottom of the chart K until RC 368 then rep from the bottom of the chart again until RC 492. Cast on 3 sts at LT edge. Cont until 2nd rep of chart RC 736 and then commence 3rd pattern rep and K until 175 R. RC 911.
Set carr to knit. Using MY, K 6 R. TD 10, K 1 R. TD 5, K 6 R. Turn up welt

by picking up first row and re-hanging onto N. Bind off.

RIGHT PANEL

Knit as for LT panel, but read chart from top down, and rep.
At RC 492, cast on 3 sts at RT side. Complete with welt as before.

MAKING UP

With RT sides of work facing pick up sts from welt at bound off edge to 3 sts cast on at side edge of both panels. K 1 R and bind off using 2 col as foll. Bind off first st with MY then bind off 2nd st with 2 ends of cream. Cont like this with alt col until all sts are bound off. (For binding off, use 2 ends of CY throughout.)

Side Welts
Left Panel
Starting at front outer edge of the LT panel (as garment is worn), with RT side facing, pick up alt loops down side, and hang onto 200 N.
K welt as for ends of panels and bind off with MY and green on alt sts as before.
Rehang next 200 loops and complete as before using MY and gold to bind off.
Rehang remaining loops and bind off using MY and cream.

Right Panel
Complete as for LT side but using MY and green for first 200 N, MY and red for 2nd 200 N and MY and black for remaining N when binding off.

Left Front Edge
Pick up 200 sts, and work welt as before, binding off with MY and black.

Right Front Edge
Work as for LT front edge but bind off with MY and cream.

Neck Edge
Pick up 180 sts around neck edge from welt to welt and K welt. Bind off using MY and green.
Darn in loose ends. Give final light pressing and steaming.

Worked in one color, the wrap is less time-consuming to knit.

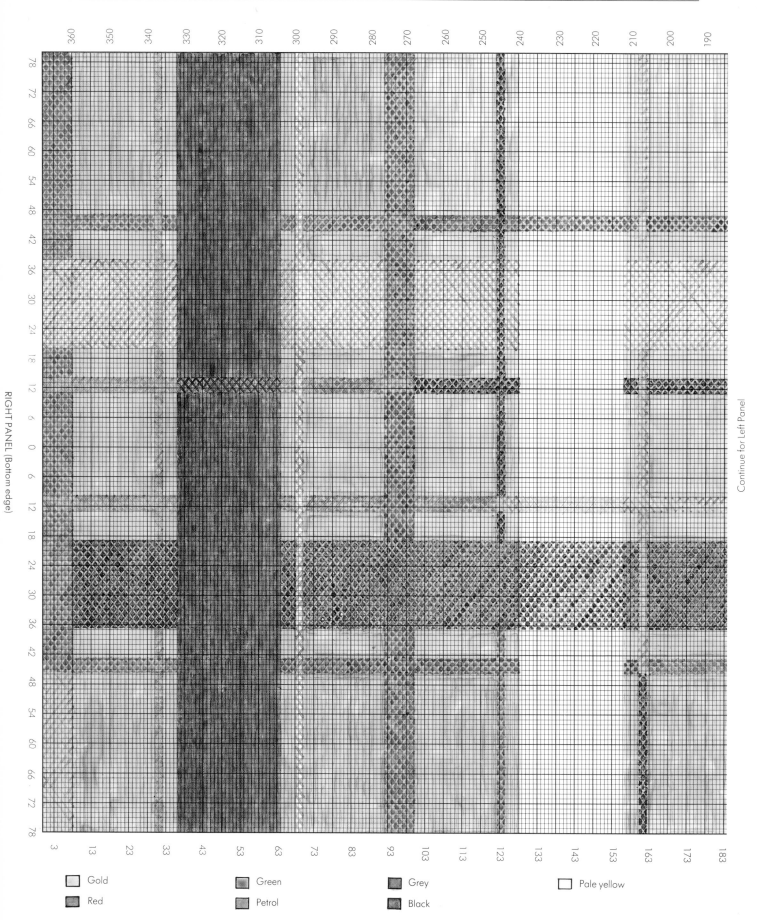

RIGHT PANEL (Bottom edge)

Continue for Left Panel

Gold

Red

Green

Petrol

Grey

Black

Pale yellow

LEFT PANEL (Bottom edge)

Continue for Right Panel

000 010 020 030 040 050 060 070 080 090 100 110 120 130 140 150 160 170 180

193 203 213 223 233 243 253 263 273 283 293 303 313 323 333 343 353 363

78 72 66 60 54 48 42 36 30 24 18 12 6 0 6 12 18 24 30 36 42 48 54 60 66 72 78

Use gray, black and pale yellow as
base yarns, weaving with all colors
as shown in the chart.

CREAM SUIT

The combination of a fitted straight skirt and three-quarter length jacket make up this tailored suit. The tuck stitch gives slightly more body so that the suit keeps its shape well. Good alternative fabrics for this suit would be a slip stitch or Fair Isle – a classic combination being a pinstripe Fair Isle (page 26) or herringbone slip stitch (page 38).

This suit is suitable for knitters with a little experience, and may be knitted on all single and double bed machines with patterning facility. Read through the pattern completely before starting to knit.

SIZES

(Figures for larger sizes are given in square brackets)

Skirt
To fit 61[66:71:76]cm/24[26:28:30]in waist
86[91:97:102]cm/34[36:38:40]in hip
66cm/26in in length

Finished measurements

Waist	66[71:76:81]cm/	26[28:30:32]in
Hips	91[97:102:107]cm/	36[38:40:42]in
Length	66cm/26in	

Jacket
To fit 86[91:97:102]cm/34[36:38:40]in chest

Finished measurements

Chest	106[112:117:122]cm/	42[44:46:48]in
Length	69cm/27½in	
Sleeve	49cm/19in	

MATERIALS

Rowan Botany Wool in cream
Skirt:
400g/14½oz all sizes
Jacket:
750g/26½oz all sizes
1 × 20cm (8in) lightweight skirt zipper in color to match.

GAUGE

MG = 29 sts and 96 R to 10cm (4in) sq TD approx 2 ∞ for main fabric
Please match gauge accurately before commencing the garments.

PATTERN NOTES

The purl side of the fabric is used as the right side throughout. All inc and dec are worked with a 6 trans tool unless otherwise stated.
Certain makes of machine are capable of tucking in one row, then knitting in the opposite direction. If your machine is of this type, use punchcard 1; if not, then use punchcard 2 (page 137).

SKIRT FRONT

Push up 132[140:148:154] N. Using WY cast on. K 10 R. Change to MY. RC 000. Set to MG and carr to knit. K 6 R str.
TD 6, K 1 R, TD to MG, K 6 R.
Turn up welt placing first row of sts in MY onto N. Unravel WY.
Set carr to tuck, and insert appropriate card acccording to machine type. (See Pattern Notes.) RC 000.
K str to RC 460.
Dec 1 st on both sides of work, K 8 R, 19 times altogether. RC 612. K 8 R. RC 620.

Knit waistband on
∗∗ Change carr to knit. K 24 R at MG. TD 6, K 1 R. TD MG, K 24 R.
Pick up first row of st st, and rehang onto N. Bind off both together with MY.∗∗

SKIRT BACK

K as for Front to RC 540. Bring all N to LT of center to HP, and set to knit RT side only. Make note of row number in card window. Cont with shaping to RC 620.
RC 000. K waistband as for Front from ∗∗ to ∗∗.
Turn card back to noted number.

Return N in HP to WP. K second side reversing shapings.

MAKING UP

Join side seams and waistband seams. Set zipper into skirt and waistband. Give final light pressing.

JACKET BACK

Push up 152[160:168:176] N. ∗Using WY cast on. K 20 R. Change to MY. TD at MG. RC 000.
Carr set to knit. K 8 R.
TD 6, K 1 R. TD at MG K 8 R.
Turn up welt as for Skirt. RC 000.
Insert card, set machine to K patt as Skirt.∗ K to RC 400.

Armhole Shaping
Dec 1 st ff both ends of work, K 4 R, 10 times altogether. RC 440. K str to RC 596.
132[140:148:156] sts rem.

Shoulder Shaping
Set carr to hold.
At side opposite carr place 5[5:6:6] N to HP on next 2 R, K 3 more R. (5 R knitted in all.) Rep 5 times more. RC 626. 60[68:76:84] sts rem in WP.
Continue shoulder shaping, and at the same time make back neck shaping.
At RC 626, K 3 R. Note number in punchcard window.
Using odd length of MY, bind off center 36 sts. Bring all rem N at LT of center to HP, and work on RT side only.
Dec ff 1 st at neck edge on alt R, 4 times altogether.
Cont with shoulder shaping until last 4[8:4:8] N in HP. RC 638.
Return N on RT to WP. K 2 R st st. Change to WY. K 10 R, release from machine.
Rep for opposite side, reversing shapings.

RIGHT JACKET FRONT

(Knit two reversing shapings)
Push up 81[85:89:93] N. Foll Back
instructions from * to *.
K str to RC 290.
*Commence lapel shaping at RT
edge.*
Inc 1 st ff every 17th R, 10 times
altogether. RC 460.
Dec 1 st ff, every 24th R, 3 times. At
the same time at RC 400 commence
armhole shaping. Dec 1 st ff at LT
edge of work, K 4 R 10 times
altogether. Cont with lapel shaping
until RC 532.
Commence neck shaping. Use single
trans tool, and work at edge of work.
Dec 1 st every 2nd R, 2 times. RC 536.
Dec 1 st every R 32 times. RC 568. At
RC 596, *commence shoulder shaping.*
Set carr to hold. At shoulder push
5[5:6:6] N to HP, K 4 R, then push
5[5:6:6] N to HP, K 6 R. Cont shoulder
shaping in this way, but keeping neck
edge str.
At completion of shoulder shaping,
RC 638, return N to WP, K 2 R st st.
Change to WY, K 10 R, release from
machine.

LEFT JACKET FRONT

K as for right Front but reversing all
shapings.

JACKET BINDING

With RT side of work facing you, pick
up center edge of Front. Using MY,
and st K 5 R at MG. Bind off. Rep for
opposite Front.

SLEEVE

(Knit two alike)
Push up 80 N. Follow instructions for
Back from * to *.
Inc 1 st ff both sides, K 14 R, 29 times
altogether. K 12 R str. RC 418. 138 sts
rem. Dec 1 st ff both sides, K 3 R, 12
times. RC 454. 114 sts rem. Bind off.

COLLAR

Push up 94 N. Cast on with MY using
e-wrap method. Set machine to knit
tuck fabric as Skirt.
Inc 1 st ff both sides, K 2 R, 15 times.

RC 30. 124 sts rem. K 4 R str.
Dec 1 st ff both sides, K 2 R, 5 times.
Push center 66 sts to HP and push all
N at LT of center to HP. Work on RT
side only.

Edge and Center Shaping

***Dec 1 st, K 2 R, 5 times at edge of
collar. *At the same time* at center,
push 2 N to HP every R, 9 times.***
Push all rem N this side to HP. Work
on opposite side rep from *** to ***
reversing shapings.
Return all N to WP. K 1 R st st.
Bind off.

BREAST POCKET

Push up 30 N. Using e-wrap, cast on
in MY. K 2 R st st. Set for tuck patt. K
88 R str. Change to st st. K welt as for
Skirt. Bind off.

LARGE POCKETS

(Knit two alike)
Push up 44 N, and cast on as for
breast pocket. K 126 R. Change to st
st. K welt, bind off.

MAKING UP

Rehang RT shoulder sections of Back
and Fronts onto machine, with
wrong sides facing. Unravel WY. Bind
off together.
Rep for LT shoulder.
Sew in sleeves. Join sleeve seams,
and side seams. Sew on collar.
With tuck side of fabric facing you,
rehang collar, and tops of lapels
onto N. Set carr to knit, and MG.
K 5 R. Bind off.
Position pocket on garment and sew
in place. Give final light pressing.

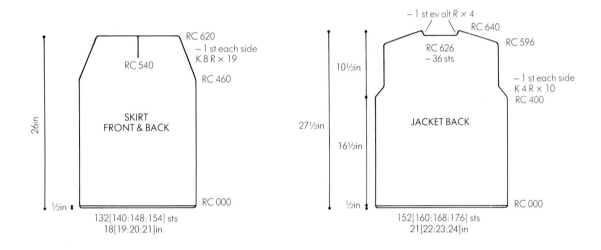

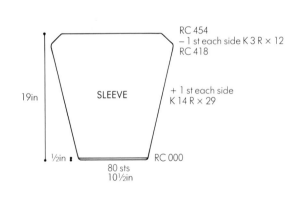

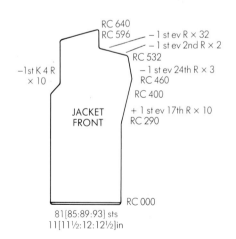

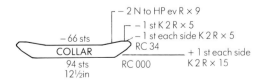

BREAST POCKET

SIDE POCKET

DRESSY SWEATER

The look of this sweater can be altered by the choice of yarn and the selection of collar. The sweater is knitted in 3-ply cashmere, but it would be just as attractive in 100% lambswool. The shirt collar and the tie are set onto yokes which are worn inside the neckline.

This pattern is suitable for all knitters, and may be knitted on all standard gauge machines, with a ribber fitted. If you do not have a ribber, knit welts by the hand method (page 124). Please read through the pattern completely before beginning to knit.

SIZES

(Figures for larger sizes are given in square brackets)
To fit 86[91:97:102]cm/34[36:38:40]in chest

Finished measurements
Chest   103[108:114:120]cm/
               40½[42½:45:47]in
Length   64cm/25in
Sleeve length 48cm/19in

MATERIALS

400g/14½oz Todd & Duncan 3-ply Cashmere in pink frost all sizes sweater
150g/5½oz both tie and shirt yokes

GAUGE

MG = 28 sts and 45 R to 10cm (4in) sq
TD approx 6 for main fabric
TD approx 2-3 for welt
Please match gauges accurately before commencing garment. Swatch should be washed, dried, and steamed before taking measurements.

PATTERN NOTES

The knit side of the fabric is used as the right side throughout. Inc and dec are worked with single tool. Yarn is taken singly throughout pattern. This garment has several additional yokes made to wear with the sweater, giving varied neckline interest.

Each yoke is knitted separately, working the yoke back and front in one piece.

BACK

Push up 142[150:158:166] N on both beds, and arrange for 1 × 1 welt. Using MY, and tightest G possible, cast on. RC 000.
Set to Rib G, and K 40 R.
Trans all sts to back bed. RC 000. Set machine to knit, and TD 6. K to RC 126 str.

Shape Armhole
Dec 1 st both ends next 14 R. RC 140. 114[122:130:138] sts rem.
K str to RC 242.

Back Neck Shaping
Using an odd length of MY, bind off center 32 sts.
Place LT side N into HP, and work on RT side only.
At LT edge, dec 1 st every R, 5 times. K 1 R. 36[40:44:48] sts rem. RC 248.
Change to WY. K 10 R, release from machine. Rep for opposite side reversing shapings.

FRONT

Work as for Back to RC 204.

Front Neck Shaping
Using odd length of MY, bind off center 24 sts. Place all N at LT of center into HP. Work on RT side first.
Dec 1 st at neck edge on alt R, 7 times. RC 234.
38[42:46:50] sts rem. K 4 R.
Dec 1 st at neck edge, K 5 R, twice. 36[40:44:48] sts rem. RC 232. K str to RC 248.
Rehang corresponding Back shoulder onto N. Remove WY. Bind off both sections together. Rep shaping for opposite side, reversing shapings. Remove onto WY.

Neck Binding
Hang neckline onto N evenly, with right side facing you. K 6 R at MG,

then bind off evenly.
Rehang LT shoulder sections onto machine with wrong sides together. Remove WY. Bind off together.

SLEEVES

(Knit two alike)
Push up 64 N on both beds, and arrange for 1 × 1 welt. Using MY, cast on as for Back and Front, and K 40 R at Rib G.
Trans all sts to back bed. Set machine to knit, and MG.
Inc 1 st both ends of next 12 R. RC 12. 88 sts rem.
Inc 1 st both ends next, and every foll 3rd row, 44 times. RC 144, 176 sts rem.
K to RC 156 str. Dec 1 st both ends K 2 R, 12 times. RC 180. 152 sts rem.
Bind off.

ADDITIONAL YOKES

(Knit 1 yoke for each collar type you choose)
Push up 112 N, and using MY cast on by e-wrap method. Set machine to knit, and for MG. K 49 R str.
Using odd length of MY, bind off 20 sts in center. Push LT side N to HP, and work at RT only first.
At neck edge, dec 1 st, K 2 R, 5 times. RC 59. Dec 1 st, K 4 R, twice. RC 67. K 8 R. RC 75. 39 sts rem. Inc 1 st at neck edge, K 1 R.
Push all N this side to HP.
Work on opposite side, returning those N to WP, reversing shapings from * to *.
Using MY, e-wrap cast on center 32 sts. Return all N to WP. K 65 R str.
Bind off.

TIE COLLAR

Cast on with e-wrap over 40 N. K 280 R at MG in st st. Bind off.
Hand sew to yoke, leaving 7.5cm (3in) gap at Front center.

SHIRT COLLAR

Push up 116 N on back bed only. Cast on using e-wrap method. Set machine to knit and MG.

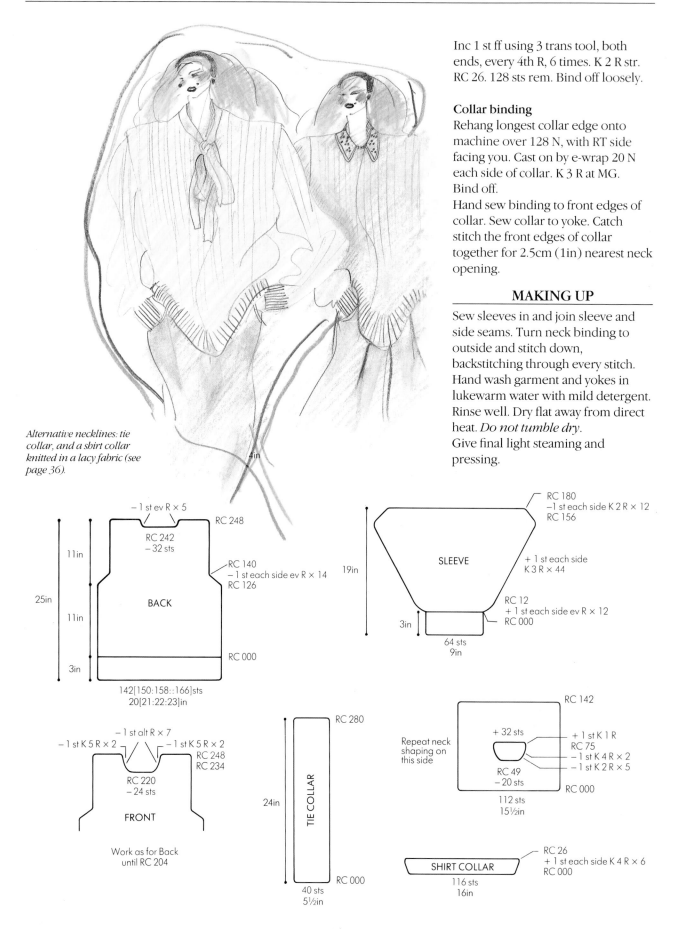

Inc 1 st ff using 3 trans tool, both ends, every 4th R, 6 times. K 2 R str. RC 26. 128 sts rem. Bind off loosely.

Collar binding
Rehang longest collar edge onto machine over 128 N, with RT side facing you. Cast on by e-wrap 20 N each side of collar. K 3 R at MG. Bind off.
Hand sew binding to front edges of collar. Sew collar to yoke. Catch stitch the front edges of collar together for 2.5cm (1in) nearest neck opening.

MAKING UP

Sew sleeves in and join sleeve and side seams. Turn neck binding to outside and stitch down, backstitching through every stitch. Hand wash garment and yokes in lukewarm water with mild detergent. Rinse well. Dry flat away from direct heat. *Do not tumble dry.*
Give final light steaming and pressing.

Alternative necklines: tie collar, and a shirt collar knitted in a lacy fabric (see page 36).

BACK

− 1 st ev R × 5
RC 248
RC 242
− 32 sts
RC 140
− 1 st each side ev R × 14
RC 126
11in
11in
3in
25in
RC 000
142[150:158::166]sts
20[21:22:23]in

SLEEVE

RC 180
− 1 st each side K 2 R × 12
RC 156
+ 1 st each side K 3 R × 44
RC 12
+ 1 st each side ev R × 12
RC 000
19in
3in
64 sts
9in

FRONT

− 1 st alt R × 7
− 1 st K 5 R × 2
− 1 st K 5 R × 2
RC 248
RC 234
RC 220
− 24 sts
Work as for Back until RC 204

TIE COLLAR

RC 280
24in
40 sts
5½in
RC 000

RC 142
+ 32 sts
+ 1 st K 1 R
RC 75
− 1 st K 4 R × 2
− 1 st K 2 R × 5
RC 49
− 20 sts
RC 000
Repeat neck shaping on this side
112 sts
15½in

SHIRT COLLAR
RC 26
+ 1 st each side K 4 R × 6
RC 000
116 sts
16in

CABLE CARDIGAN

The cable changes size in this classic cardigan as it progresses from the rib up the fabric and it is also used to form edging detail. It could easily be adapted to a sweater or sleeveless slipover.

This pattern is suitable for knitters with a moderate amount of experience. It can be knitted on all single bed standard gauge machines with a ribber and also on most double bed machines. Please read through the pattern completely before starting to knit.

SIZES

(Figures for larger sizes are given in square brackets)
To fit 86[91:97:102]cm/34[36:38:40]in chest

Finished measurements
Chest   114[119:124:127]cm/
              45[47:49:50]in
Length   66cm/26in
Sleeve length 48cm/19in

MATERIALS

550g/19½oz Rowan Botany Wool in cream
9 small shank buttons

GAUGE

MG = 32 sts and 42 R to 10cm (4in) sq
TD approx 8 for main fabric
TD approx 3 for welts; 0 ∞for welt cast on

PATTERN NOTES

The purl side of the fabric is used as the right side throughout. All ribs are cabled as you knit as foll:
Needle set-up: top row is back bed and lower row is front bed (ribber).

| = needle in WP
● = needle in NWP
K 2 rows. Work cable as below. Using single trans tools, trans all sts marked a to N marked b, and sts marked b to N marked a, over the whole bed. (Note that cable starts and finishes one pair of needles from each end.) Rep from * to * throughout welt.

MAIN CABLE PATTERN

Starting at the LT edge, skip 2 N, and commence patt. Cross sts b over a.
LT edge | | | | | | | | | | | |
           a b   a b
(Largest size on 200 N, commence cables on N 9 and 10 from LT edge and then as above.)
K 2 R, and rep cabling, 4 times in all. RC 8. K 2 R str.

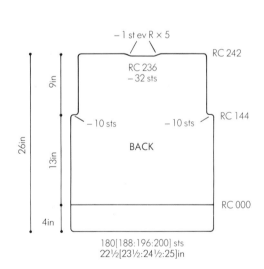

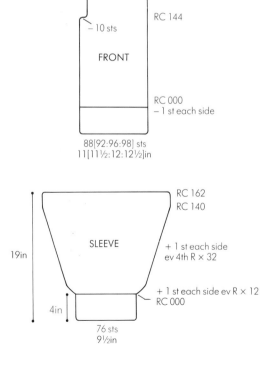

95

*** Cross N b over a. (Use 2-prong tools this time.)

LT edge | | | | | | | | |
          a a b b

K 4 R, and rep cabling, 3 times in all. RC 22.

K 2 R str. Cross N b over a. (Use 3-prong tools this time.)

LT edge | | | | | | | | | | | | | | | |
       a a a b b b   a a a b b b

K 6 R, and rep cabling, K 4 R, rep cabling. K 6 R. RC 40

Cross N b over a with 2-prong tools.

LT edge | | | | | | | | |
         a a b b

K 4 R. Rep cabling, K 2 R. Rep cabling, K 4 R. RC 50.

Cross N b over a with 1-prong tools.

LT edge | | | | | | | | |
         a b

K 2 R. Rep cabling, 8 times in all.***
RC 66.

Rep patt from *** to ***. These 56 R repeated throughout garment form the pattern.

BACK

Push up 180[188:196:200] N on both beds. Arrange in 2 × 1 setting for welt as foll:

| | • | | • | | • | | • | | • | | • | |
| | • | | • | | • | | • | | • | | • | |

Using MY, and both carr set to knit, K 1 R.

Set carr for circular knitting, K 2 R.

Rack front bed 1 place to RT according to diagram.

| | • | | • | | • | | • | | • | | • |
• | | • | | • | | • | | • | | • | | • |

K 40 rows in welt, cabling welt according to Pattern Notes.

Trans all sts to back bed. RC 000.

Set carr for knit.

TD to MG and K to RC 144 according to cable patt sequence in Pattern Notes.

Armhole Shaping

Bind off 10 sts beg next 2 R. Cont in cable sequence, and also work a small b-over-a cable on N 2 and 3 from each end, crossing every 2 R. K str to RC 236.

Keeping cable sequence correct, commence.

Back Neck Shaping

Using an odd length of MY, bind off center 32 sts. Place all N to LT of center to HP. Work RT side first, keeping patt sequnce.

Using 6-prong trans tool, at neck edge, dec 1 st every row, 5 times, K 1 R. RC 242. (Leave plain those sts that you cannot cable.)

Change to WY. K 20 R str. Release from machine.

Rep on opposite side reversing shapings.

FRONTS

(Knit two, reversing shapings)

Push up 88[92:96:98] N on both beds, and arrange for 2 × 1 welt. K to RC 40 foll welt instructions for Back and cabling.

Trans all sts to back bed. Dec 1 st each end of R. 86[90:94:96] sts rem. RC 000. Set carr to knit.

K in cable patt sequence according to Pattern Notes to RC 144.

Armhole Shaping

At RT side, bind off 10 sts. Cable up this edge as for Back patt. K to RC 201 str. Carr at LT.

Front Neck Shaping

At LT side, bind off 8 sts.

Dec 1 st every 4th R, 9 times altogether, using 6-prong trans tool. RC 237. K 5 R str.

Change to WY, K 20 R. Release from machine.

SLEEVES

(Knit two alike)

Push up 76 N on both beds, and arrange for 2 × 1 welt. Cast on and K welt according to instructions given for Back. K to RC 40.

Trans all sts to back bed. TD to MG. Carr set to st st. RC 000.

Follow instructions for cable sequence given in Pattern Notes, but work patt from center out to edges, rather than starting at LT edge.

K in this sequence keeping patt correct throughout.

Make a-over-b cable at edges every 2 R on N 2 and 3.

Using 3-prong trans tool, inc 1 st ff both ends of next 12 R, then every 4th R 32 times altogether. 164 sts rem. RC 140. K to RC 162.

Bind off.

MAKING UP

Block and steam each part to size. *Do not press as this will flatten the cable patt.*

With right sides facing, rehang back shoulder and corresponding front onto machine. Remove WY. Bind off Back and Front sections together. Rep for opposite shoulder.

Join sleeves to armhole. Sew side and underarm seams.

BANDS

Button Band

** Push up 156 N on both beds.

Arrange for 2 × 1 welt. Using MY, make closed edge cast on. Set to Rib G.** K 14 R.

Trans all sts to back bed. MG, K 1 R. With RT side of work facing you, rehang RT front onto N evenly. K 1 R. Bind off all sts.

Buttonhole Band

Rep as above from ** to **. K 5 R. Counting from RT on back bed only, make buttonholes at N 7-8 from each end and a further 7 buttonholes evenly spaced in between.

Buttonholes made as foll:

Trans 1 st from front bed to adjacent N, and 1 from back bed to adjacent N. K 9 R. Rehang RT front onto N, with RT side facing you. MG K 1 R. Bind off.

Sew buttons onto opposite band to correspond with buttonholes.

Give final light pressing.

Neck Band

Push up 136 sts both beds. Arrange for 2 × 1 welt. Using MY make closed edge cast on. Set to Rib G, K 14 R.

Trans all sts to back bed. MG K 1 R. Rehang neckline evenly on N, including tops of bands, with RT side facing. MG K 1 R. Bind off.

ARGYLE SWEATER

The traditional Argyle sweater with its recognizable diamonds of color can be knitted from a punchcard as well as by the traditional method of intarsia. The punchcard is obviously a quicker method and you can add more color and detail later by Swiss darning in the spot stripes. Another way of achieving the Argyle effect is by using the holding technique (page 34). This, however, creates tiny holes around the color changes. I would advise that you add the spot stripes after you have finished the knitting to make the work less confusing.

This pattern is suitable for all knitters of moderate experience, and all machines with an intarsia carriage or facility. The sweater is designed as an oversize garment. Please read through the pattern, and study the charts before starting to knit.

SIZES

(Figures for larger sizes are given in square brackets)
To fit 86[91:96:102]cm/34[36:38:40]in chest

Finished measurements

Chest	106[112:117:122]cm/ 42[44:46:48]in
Length	78cm/31in
Sleeve length	59cm/23in

MATERIALS

600g/21½ oz Forsell 4-ply Wool in natural (MY) all sizes
50g/2oz Rowan Botany Wool in each of the following colors: rust, red, green, gold, slate, cream

GAUGE

MG = 33 sts and 43 R to 10cm (4in) sq.
TD approx 5 for main garment parts
Rib G approx 2 for all welts
If your machine utilizes a separate intarsia carriage, ensure the TD numbers match those of the main carr, or note number giving the correct gauge and change numerals within pattern before commencing the garment. Please match gauges accurately before commencing the garment.

PATTERN NOTES

The knit side of the fabric is used as the right side throughout. Follow intarsia charts provided for all patterning and shaping. Cross yarns where colors change to avoid hole in work (page 44).

The use of an intarsia yarn brake will greatly facilitate working this garment. All inc and dec worked on edge N throughout. The chart is drawn for the largest size. If you are making a smaller size, subtract an equal number of sts from either side so that the Argyle diamonds are centered on the garment.

BACK

Push up 175[183:191:199) N on both beds. Arrange for 1 × 1 welt. Using MY cast on. Set to Rib G, RC 000. K 40 R. Transfer all sts to back bed. Set machine for intarsia, or change to intarsia carr. Set to MG. RC 000. Foll charts for shapings and color.

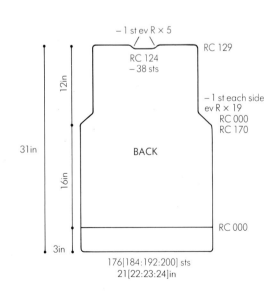

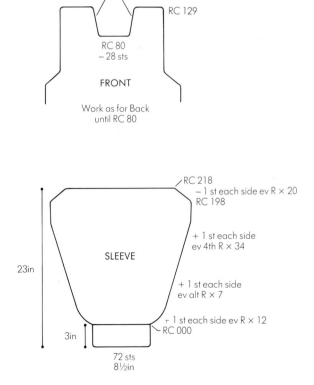

changes K to RC 170. RC 000. Dec 1 st at each end of the next 20 R. ∗ K to RC 124, bind off 38 sts at center and push all N at LT to HP, K 1 R. Dec 1 st. at neck edge ev R 5 times. Bind off rem sts. RC 129. Push N at LT to WP and complete to match RT side.

FRONT

K as for Back until ∗. K to RC 80 then bind off 28 sts at center and push all N to LT to HP. Dec 1 st at neck edge ev 5th R 9 times. K 5 R. RC 129. Bind off rem sts. Push N at LT to WP and complete to match RT side.

SLEEVES

Push up 72 N on both beds, and arrange for 1 × 1 welt. Cast on and K welt as for Back and Front. Transfer all sts to back bed. K both sleeves foll chart for shapings and col changes, and altering col arrangement of diamonds on second sleeve. Inc 1 st at both sides ev R 12 times, then ev alt R 7 times, and ev 4th R 34 times. K to RC 198. Dec 1 st at both sides ev R 20 times. Bind off rem sts.

NECK WELT

Push up 140 N on both beds, and arrange for 1 × 1 welt. Cast on as for Back and Front and K 12 R. Transfer all sts to back bed. K 1 R at MG. Change to WY. K 10 R, release from machine.

MAKING UP

Swiss darn (page 130) all fine lines on bodies and sleeves following the chart for colors. Hand sew shoulder seams. Commencing at LT shoulder, and using length of MY, backstitch neck welt to neckline, through first row of loops in MY (page 129). Unravel WY as you go. Join neck seam at LT. Sew in sleeves, and join side seams. Give final light pressing.

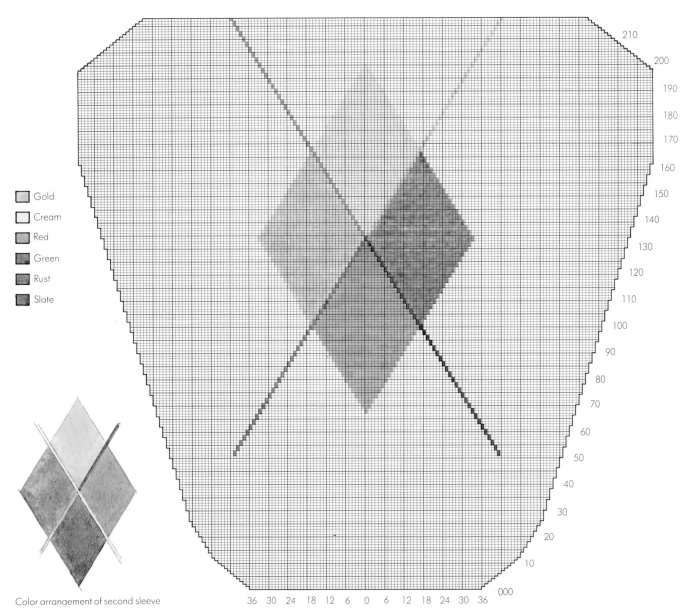

Gold
Cream
Red
Green
Rust
Slate

Color arrangement of second sleeve

210
200
190
180
170
160
150
140
130
120
110
100
90
80
70
60
50
40
30
20
10
000

36 30 24 18 12 6 0 6 12 18 24 30 36

SLEEVE

FRONT/BACK

GANSEY SUIT

The textured diamonds and the detailed finishing at the seams on this suit are inspired by traditional fishermen's sweaters. All the motifs are worked with hand texture techniques which open up a whole new dimension by extending machine knitting for those with or without rib attachments. The skirt is constructed from five identical panels and all the pieces are grafted together on the machine, which accentuates the seaming with a chain.

A simplified suit could be worked in plain knitting or using alternative motifs taken from traditional knitting sources. Even though this suit is extremely time-consuming to knit, it is still more realistic to create such a garment on a machine than by hand.

SIZES

(Figures for larger sizes are given in square brackets)

Cardigan
To fit 86[91:96:102]cm/34[36:38:40]in chest

Finished measurements
Chest   99[104:109:114]cm/
             39[41:43:45]in
Length   62cm/24½in
Sleeve length 49.5cm/19½in

Skirt
To fit 63.5[66:68.5:71]cm/
25[26:27:28]in waist

Finished measurements
Waist   81[84:86:89]cm/
         32[33:34:35]in
Length   79cm/35in
If you require any other length, add or subtract R from after the last diamond, but remember to consider the fit at the hip.

MATERIALS

Forsell 4-ply Wool in natural
Cardigan
550g/19½ oz all sizes
9 × 2cm (¾in) buttons
Skirt
750g/26½oz all sizes
2.5cm (1in) elastic

GAUGE

MG = 34 sts and 44 R to 10cm (4in) sq
TD approx 5
TD for rib approx 3

PATTERN NOTES

Knit side of the fabric is right side and all inc are made by trans 6 sts outwards 1 st and filling the empty N with the purl loop from the next st. A further inc is made on the edge of the short ribs on the Back and Front by trans sts marked on chart 1 N to LT or RT and filling empty N with purl loops from next st. All dec are worked in the same way by trans 6 sts inwards. If not using a ribber, the 2 × 2 rib is worked by using a hand cast on, knit the correct number of rows for the rib and then use the latch tool. Drop every 3rd and 4th st down to the cast on and latch the sts back up the other way to form a purl st. All the purl sts on the chart are worked in this way.
The decorative eyelet detail is worked by moving 6 sts on the center side of short rib 1 st outwards or inwards, and leaving the empty N still in WP.

CARDIGAN BACK

Push up 136[144:152:160] N to WP and either cast on by hand on the back bed if you are not using a ribber (see Pattern Notes), or arrange the N for 2 × 2 rib if using a ribber. K 50 R. Trans all N to back bed and commence patt foll chart.
Inc 2 sts across both sides every 5th R 7 times (i.e. inc 1 st on edge side of short rib and inc 1 st at side edge).

See Pattern Notes.
164[172:180:188] sts.
K to RC 118. Bind off 9 sts at the beg of the next 2 R. K to RC 208.

Shape Back Neck
Bind off 26 sts at center and push all N at LT to HP. Dec 1 st at neck edge every R 11 times by moving 6 sts outwards each R. K 5 R. RC 224. Put rem sts onto WY. Push all N at RT to WP and complete to match RT side.

FRONTS

(Knit 2, reversing shapings)
Push up 63[67:71:75] N to WP and K rib as for Back and commence patt from chart. Working inc at one side only (see Pattern Notes), K to RC 118. Bind off 9 sts at side edge. K to RC 170.

Neck Shaping
Bind off 7 sts at center front then dec 1 st on the next and every foll 4th R 12 times by moving 6 sts outwards. K to RC 224.

SLEEVES

(Knit 2 alike)
Push up 85 N to WP and work 38 R of rib as for Back and commence patt from chart. All inc are worked as for Back. Inc 1 st both ends every 3rd R 9 times, then both ends every 4th R 28 times. K 10 R then inc 1 st again each side. 161 sts. K to RC 176, put sts onto WY.

BANDS

Neckband
Push up 160 N to WP and K 10 R 2 × 2 rib. Put onto WY.

Buttonhole Band
Push up 166 N to WP and K 10 R 2 × 2 rib making 9 evenly spaced buttonholes by binding off 2 sts on R 5 and casting on 2 sts on R 6. Put onto WY.

Button Band

Work as for Buttonhole band but omitting buttonholes.

MAKING UP

Join shoulders by hooking sts from each shoulder onto N with wrong sides tog. K 1 R then bind off taking st around gate pegs. This forms a bind off chain on the RT side of garment. Join sleeve to main garment by hooking up sts from armholes onto N with wrong side facing, place center of armhole onto center N omitting 9 sts at armhole shaping. With RT side facing, hook up sts from sleeve onto the same N, placing 2 sts onto 30 N each side of center and 1 st onto rem N. K 1 R and bind off around gate pegs. Sew 9 sts by hand to sleeve seam.

Join side seam by hooking sts onto N evenly with wrong side tog and binding off in the same way.

Join neck rib to garment by hooking neck of garment onto machine with wrong side facing (110 sts approx). Hook sts from neck rib onto N, placing 2 purl sts from rib onto 1 N and 1 K st onto 1 N. K 1 R and bind off around gate pegs. Join front ribs in the same way. Sew in all ends and press thoroughly. Sew on buttons.

SKIRT PANELS

Push up 175[177:179:181] N to WP on both beds and arrange for 2 × 2 rib and K 8 R as on the cardigan. Trans all N to back bed. Commence patt foll chart and at RC 10 dec 1 st at both sides every 5th R using the same method as on the cardigan until 59[61:63:65] sts rem. RC 295. Work 3 sts horizontal rib over the center of last diamond and cont 2 ribs either side until RC 398. Put work onto WY.

K another 4 panels the same, 5 in total.

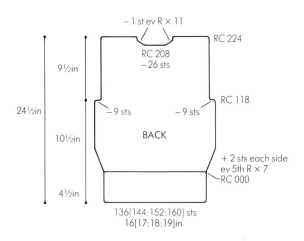

− 1 st ev R × 11
RC 224
RC 208
− 26 sts
RC 118
9½in
24½in
− 9 sts   − 9 sts
BACK
10½in
+ 2 sts each side ev 5th R × 7
RC 000
4½in
136[144:152:160] sts
16[17:18:19]in

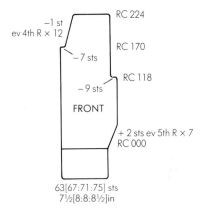

RC 224
−1 st ev 4th R × 12
RC 170
− 7 sts
RC 118
− 9 sts
FRONT
+ 2 sts ev 5th R × 7
RC 000
63[67:71:75] sts
7½[8:8:8½]in

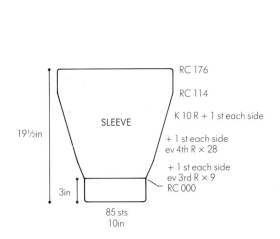

RC 176
RC 114
K 10 R + 1 st each side
19½in
SLEEVE
+ 1 st each side ev 4th R × 28
+ 1 st each side ev 3rd R × 9
RC 000
3in
85 sts
10in

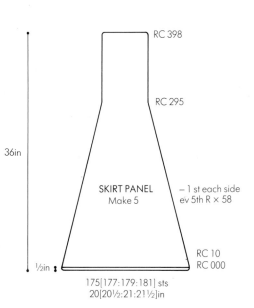

RC 398
RC 295
36in
SKIRT PANEL
Make 5
− 1 st each side ev 5th R × 58
RC 10
RC 000
½in
175[177:179:181] sts
20[20½:21:21½]in

WAISTBAND

Pick up sts from 1 panel and put onto
N with RT side facing. K 11 R TD 5, K
3 R TD 3, and K 11 R TD 5. Pick up sts
from first R and work 1 R TD. Bind
off around gate pegs. Complete the
other 4 panels the same.

MAKING UP

Press panels lightly and join them tog
using the same method as for
cardigan but using 2 ends of yarn to
bind off around gate pegs. You will
have to join the panel seams in 2
operations. Hook up the first 200 sts
onto N and bind off these and then,
without breaking off yarn, hook up
rem sts and bind off these sts.
Hand graft waistband tog leaving 1
seam open, insert elastic and close
opening after joining elastic with flat
seam. Sew in all ends and press
thoroughly.

Purl

Trans st 1 N to LT

Trans st 1 N to RT

2 sts on this N

Make st by picking up
loop of adjacent N and
placing onto empty N

Eyelet hole formed by
leaving empty N in WP

Knit

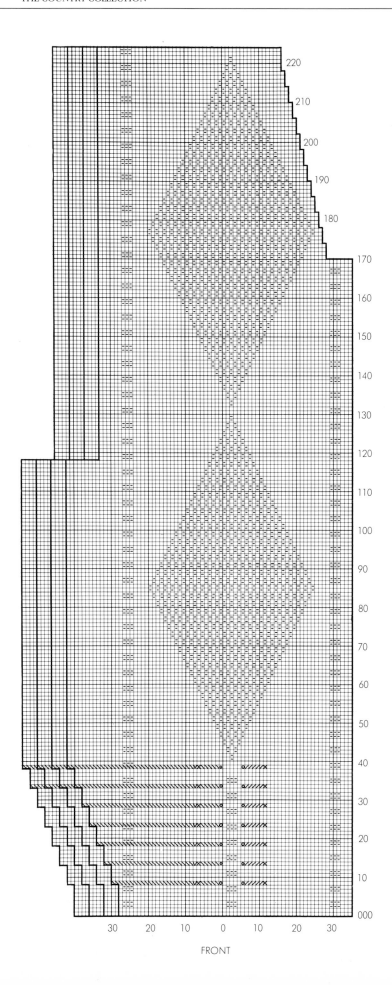

FRONT

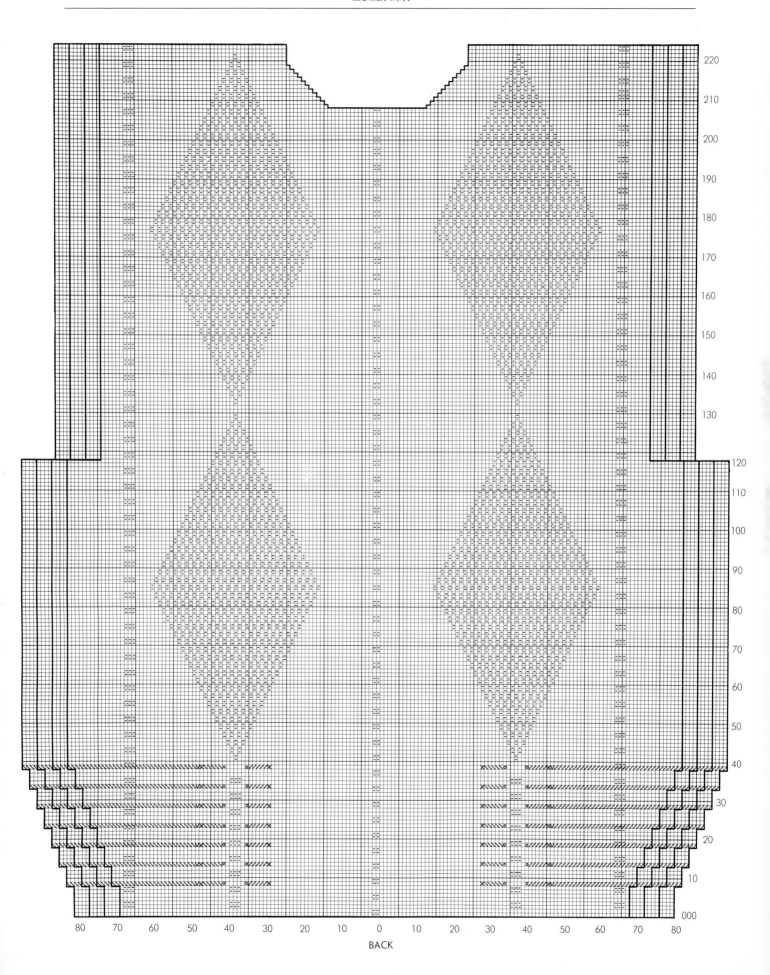

BACK

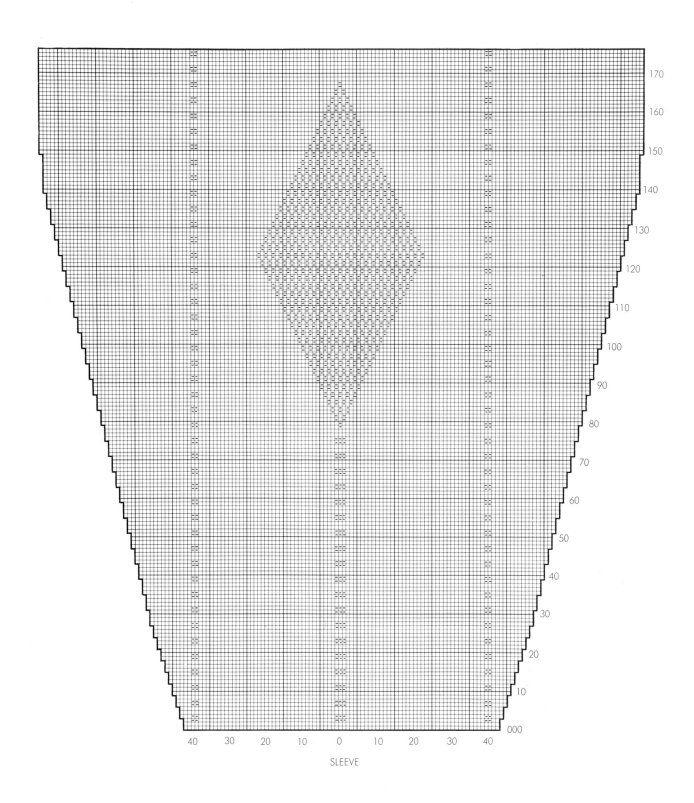

SLEEVE

Continue until RC 398

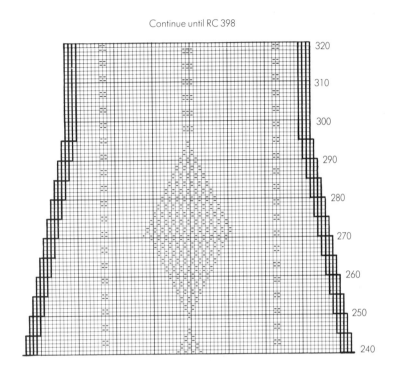

320
310
300
290
280
270
260
250
240

Continue with diamond pattern
and shaping until RC 295

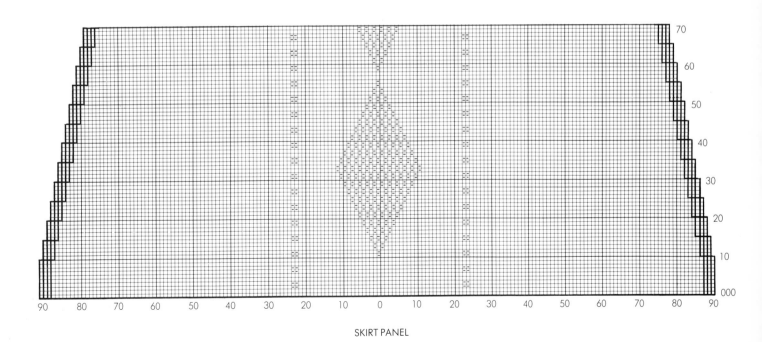

70
60
50
40
30
20
10
000

90 80 70 60 50 40 30 20 10 0 10 20 30 40 50 60 70 80 90

SKIRT PANEL

CARPET JACKET

Islamic carpets were the inspiration for this jacket which is worked in tuck stitch with isolated weaving for the colored pattern. The stitch is tucked in one direction to increase the thickness of the fabric.

The actual fabric can be altered to your own design. Just use the same number of stitches, draw up a chart the same size as the one I have given and design your own pattern for the woven shapes. More definition can be achieved by using a thicker wool, or a different fiber such as silk or cotton, to produce a contrast texture and color. You can even work the isolated weaving in one contrast color. The alternative variation replaces the zipper with a buttonband.

This pattern is suitable for knitters with some experience of knitweave techniques, and for all machines, single bed with ribber, or double bed, with a knitweave facility. Please read through the pattern completely before starting to knit.

SIZES

(Figures for larger sizes are given in square brackets)
To fit 86[91:96:102]cm/34[36:38:40]in chest

Finished measurements
Chest 111[116:122:127]cm/ 44[46:48:50]in

Length 83cm/32in
K 6 (15) R more or less for each cm (in) to lengthen or shorten garment, keeping woven pattern correct.
Sleeve length 49cm/19in

MATERIALS

750g/26½oz Forsell 4-ply Wool in natural (MY).
Rowan Botany Wool, 75g/3oz black, 50g/2oz each rust, blue, gold, red, green 1 × 72cm (28in) separating lightweight zipper in color to match (or size to fit if you have changed the garment length)
11 buttons for alternative

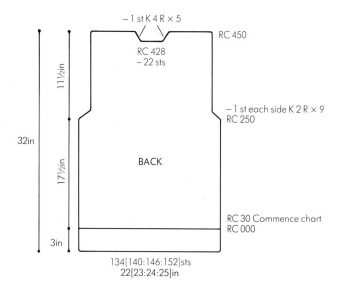

BACK

32in
11½in
17½in
3in

− 1 st K 4 R × 5
RC 450
RC 428
− 22 sts
− 1 st each side K 2 R × 9
RC 250
RC 30 Commence chart
RC 000
134[140:146:152]sts
22[23:24:25]in

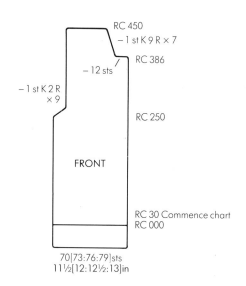

FRONT

RC 450
− 1 st K 9 R × 7
RC 386
− 12 sts
− 1 st K 2 R × 9
RC 250
RC 30 Commence chart
RC 000
70[73:76:79]sts
11½[12:12½:13]in

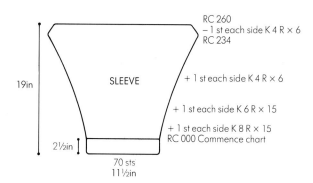

SLEEVE

19in
2½in

RC 260
− 1 st each side K 4 R × 6
RC 234
+ 1 st each side K 4 R × 6
+ 1 st each side K 6 R × 15
+ 1 st each side K 8 R × 15
RC 000 Commence chart
70 sts
11½in

COLLAR

6in
RC 78
RC 000
160 sts
26½in

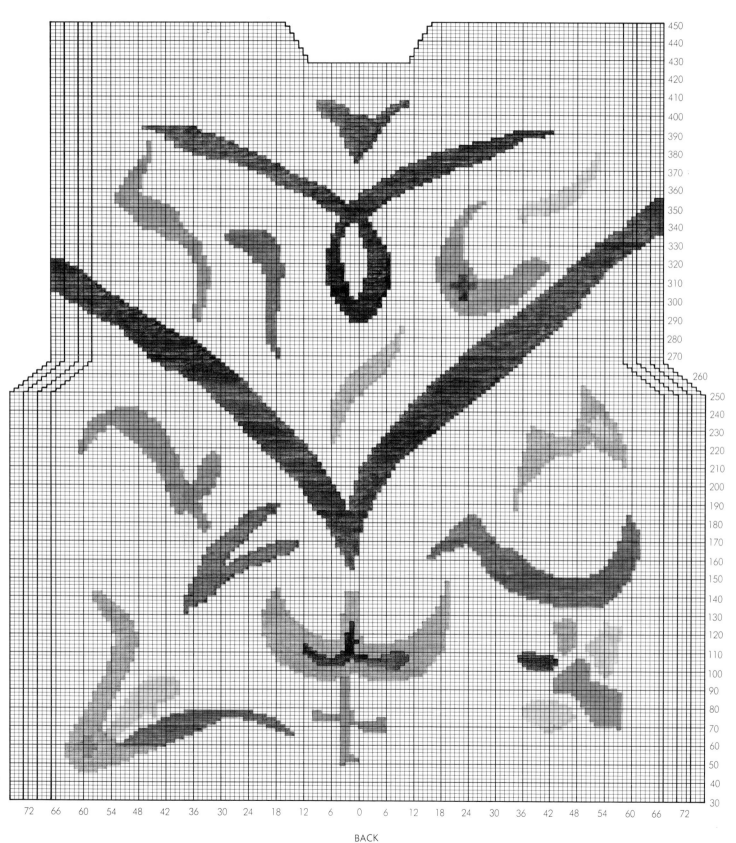

BACK

GAUGE

MG = 24 sts and 60 R to 10cm (4in) sq
TD approx 7 ○ for main fabric
Rib G approx 4
Please match gauges accurately
before commencing the garment.

PATTERN NOTES

The purl side of the fabric is used as
the right side throughout. The main
fabric of this garment is a tuck stitch,
with knitweave sections forming the
design in colors. Please follow chart
for designs. The pattern is formed
with 1 row tucking, 1 row knitting.
Knitweave using two ends of yarn is
done on the knit rows only. Some
machines knit this pattern
automatically. If your machine does
this, use punchcard 1. If not, use
punchcard 2 (page 137). Certain
machines preselect needles to UWP
for the foll row of pattern (e.g.
Japanese machines from Brother and
Toyota). In this case, place weave
yarn over needles in places
corresponding to chart. If your
machine does not select needles by
bringing them to UWP in the
previous row (e.g. Japanese
machines manufactured by Silver-
Reed, and French machines from
Superba), needles must be hand
selected to UWP in positions
corresponding to chart on *every knit
row* before weaving yarn is laid over.
The chart is for the largest size. If you
are making a smaller size, subtract an
equal number of stitches at both side
seams. The color blocks are in the
same position for all sizes.

BACK

Push up 134[140:146:152] N on both
beds, and arrange for 2 × 1 rib.
Using MY cast on and K 3 circular R,
rack front bed 1 pos to the RT. TD 4,
K 50 R. Trans all sts to back bed and
insert punchcard according to type
of machine. Set machine to tuck one
way and knit the other way. RC 000. K
to RC 30 before working from chart.
Foll weaving chart to RC 250. Dec 1 st
both sides K 2 R, 9 times. RC 268.
K str foll chart to RC 428. Using odd
length of MY, bind off center 22 sts.
*Put all N at LT of center to HP. Set
carr to hold. Knit RT side only first. At
neck edge dec 1 st K 4 R, 5 times
altogether. K 2 R st st. RC 450.
Change to WY K 20 R. Release from
machine.*
Rep from * to * reversing shapings.

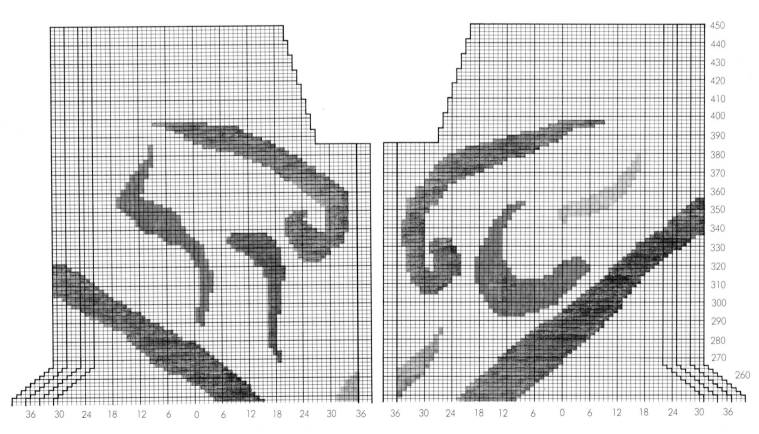

Works as for Back until RC 300

FRONT

FRONTS

(Knit two, reversing shapings)
Push up 70[73:76:79] N on both beds.
Arrange for 2 × 1 rib. K 50 R rib as
for Back and trans sts to back bed.
Work as for Back but foll chart for
Front (3 sts at center front without
weaving patt are for zipper).
K to RC 386. Bind off 12 sts at neck
edge. Dec 1 st at neck edge on next
R, K 8 R, 7 times. K 6 R, K 2 R st st. RC
450. Change to WY, K 20 R. Rehang
Back shoulder onto same N with RT
side together. Unravel WY and K 1 R
and bind off around gate pegs.
Complete other shoulder seam in
same way.

SLEEVES

(Knit two alike)
Push up 70 N on both beds. Arrange
for 2 × 1 rib. Cast on and K 36 R rib
as for Back.
Trans all sts to back bed. Set machine
for tuck patt and commence chart at
R 000.
Inc 1 st both sides, K 8 R, 15 times
altogether.
Inc 1 st both sides, K 6 R, 15 times.
Inc 1 st both sides, K 4 R, 6 times. RC
234. 142 sts rem.
Dec 1 st both sides K 4 R, 6 times. 130
sts rem.
K 2 R st st RC 260. Bind off.

COLLAR

Push up 160 N on both beds. Arrange
for 2 × 1 rib. Cast on in MY as for
Back. K 76 R. Trans all sts to back
bed. K 2 R at MG in st st. Bind off.

BANDS

Buttonhole Band

Push up 200 N to WP and K 12 R 2 ×
1 rib making 11 buttonholes evenly
spaced by binding off 2 sts on RC 5
and casting on 2 sts on RC 6. Rehang
Front onto same N, K 1 R and bind off
around gate pegs.

Button Band

Work as for Buttonhole band but
omit buttonholes. Sew on buttons.

MAKING UP

Join sleeve seams and side seams.
Sew on collar, and fold in half. Catch
down on inside. Sew in zipper.
Steam and give final light pressing.

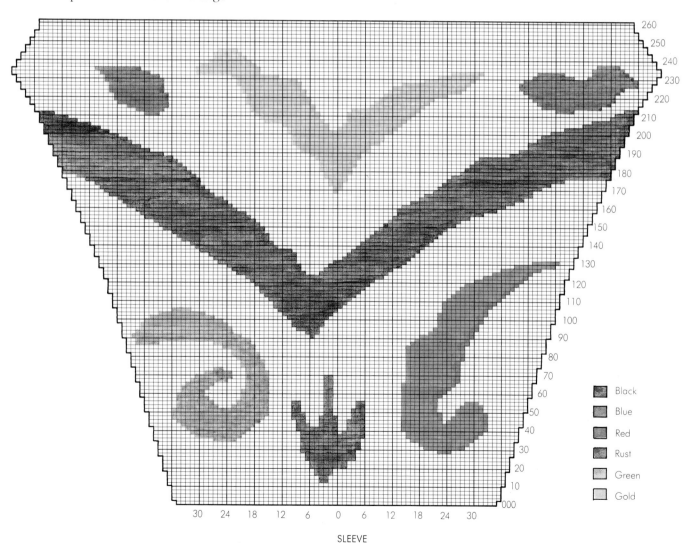

SLEEVE

TECHNICAL
INFORMATION

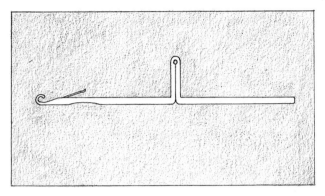

THE MACHINE page 118

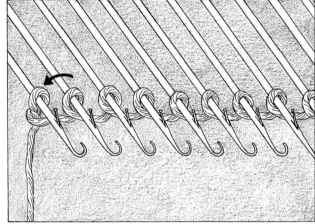

CASTING ON page 120

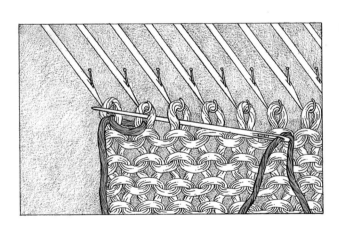

BINDING OFF page 122

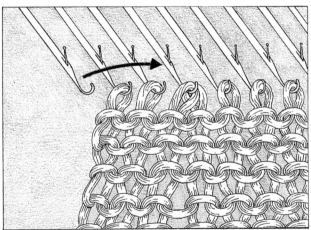

WELTS & RIBS page 124

INCREASING & DECREASING
page 126

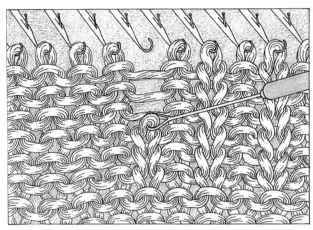

EDGES page 127

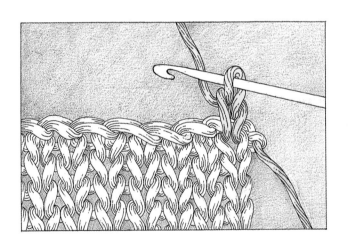

FINISHING page 128

THE MACHINE

FUNCTIONS & NEEDLE POSITIONS

There are so many different makes of machine, and each make has its own combinations of switches, levers or buttons to perform the different techniques. In order to make this book usable to all knitters I want to outline the different functions here so that knitters without manuals or a common standard machine can use this book. These are only the basic functions common to most machines.

Check through the list below (refer to your manual to save time) and mark the levers or make a list to identify which ones to use for the different techniques. Thread up your machine with waste yarn and work through the levers systematically. You need to identify whichever lever or switch on your machine affects the technique or facility.

Where needle selection is referred to, this is with the aid of a punchcard or buttons, although knitters with button machines must refer to their manuals for details on Fair Isle.

Machine settings are sometimes referred to as cam settings. If your machine does not have the facility to select needles automatically, you will need to hand select to achieve the same end.

NEEDLE POSITIONS

There are several different needle positions involved in the different techniques outlined below.

Needles pushed as far back as they will go (towards the back of the machine) are in the non-working position (NWP) where they don't knit when the carriage passes over them.

Needles that are pushed forward so that the carriage catches them when threaded with yarn – the hooks are level with the needle bed – are said to be in working position (WP).

Needles that are pulled out away from the machine as far as they will come are in holding position (HP). The carriage passes over them but the stitches do not knit. Needles that are selected to a position between WP and HP so that the latch is virtually level with the gate pegs are in upper working position (UWP), also known as patterning position. This position is usually associated with pre-selecting machines. The needles will be selected to this position for patterning either manually or by punchcard.

Pre-selecting machines
When you knit a punchcard the needles move forward to UWP.

Non-pre-selecting machines
When you knit a punchcard the needles remain in WP.

On your machine these positions may be indicated by a letter (A,B,C,D,E,F) or a number (0,1,2,3). Once you have worked out which position is which, you can follow the instructions in this book.

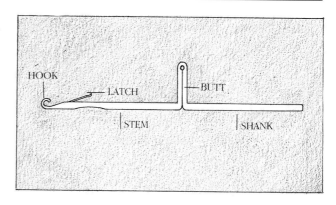

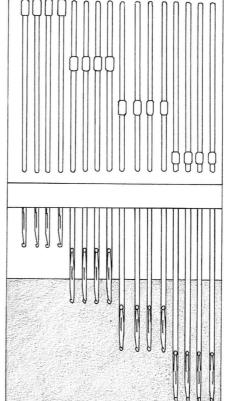

non-working position NWP

working position WP

upper working position UWP

holding position HP

FUNCTIONS CHECKLIST

The functions as defined by my patterns are given below. Refer to your manual to determine which levers or switch buttons should be engaged in order to achieve these techniques.

Fair Isle. Facility to work a second color in a pattern using needle selection, sometimes one lever is switched and both yarns are placed into the feeder (of a non-pre-selecting machine) to affect the pattern. For pre-selecting machines, the lever is engaged, the needles are selected, then the second yarn is introduced into the feeder and a second lever is engaged to tell the machine to bring in the second color.

FM = free move. The carriage moves across work on the machine with needles in WP, with or without yarn in the carriage. The machine does not knit and does not release the work from the machine. This usually involves engaging a non-knit or part lever, one for each direction, or one for both directions. This is referred to as FM or non-knit in the book.

HP = holding position. Needles brought forward to HP do not knit, with or without yarn in the carriage. Needles in WP in the same piece of work do knit. This involves engaging a hold lever or sometimes two, one for each direction. These levers can be disengaged to return needles to WP.

Intarsia. The machine knits yarn that is laid over the needles in UWP. You may have to engage a switch for this use.

Intarsia carriage. This is a small carriage that does intarsia without switching any levers. It is automatic.

Knit = stockinette stitch. The machine knits plain knitting, and selects no needles.

Knitweave. The machine works a main yarn in normal stockinette stitch but trapping a second yarn into the knitting. This usually involves engaging brushes and a weave lever.

L = large. A switch to set the punchcard so that it reads every row twice, thus enlarging the pattern. It can also stop the card and read the same line every row.

Lace carriage. A small carriage that transfers selected stitches.

Racking. A facility that moves the front bed or ribber sideways one position at a time. This is normally done with a racking handle.

Single bed Fair Isle. This is Fair Isle knitting that has floats across the work.

Slip. The yarn passes over (thus slips) the needles selected to slip, resembling a float on the reverse of a Fair Isle. This involves engaging a slip lever or sometimes two, one for each direction. Please note that the FM or non-knit lever will slip when needles are selected to UWP and FM when they are not, that is when they are in WP.

SM = single motif. This facility works one repeat of the pattern only. It can be placed in any position on some machines with the use of plastic strips placed on the needle bed, and in set positions on other machines with the use of a number dial.

Tubular. The knitting is done on one bed then the other (in the round) usually by engaging the FM button on the main carriage and a similar switch on the ribber carriage.

Tuck. The machine lays yarn in the hook of selected needles. This loop knits in on subsequent rows. This is only possible for a limited amount of rows on the same needle subject to gauge to yarn ratio, try a maximum of four to start with.

Tuck on a double bed is as for the single bed machine except all needles can be tucked on one bed if needles are being knitted on the opposite bed.

ABBREVIATIONS

alt = alternate
beg = beginning
carr = carriage(s)
ch = chain
cm = centimeter(s)
col = color
cont = continue
CY = contrast yarn
CY2 = second contrast yarn
CY3 = third contrast yarn
dec = decrease
ev = every
ff = fully fashioned
FM = free move, or non-knit
foll = following
g = gram(s)
G = gauge/stitch size
HP = holding position
in = inch(es)
inc = increas(e)(es)(ing)
K = knit
K1 P1 rib = knit one, purl one rib
LT = left
MG = main gauge
mm = millimeters
MY = main yarn
N = needle(s)
NWP = non-working position
P = purl
patt = pattern
pos = position
R = row(s)
RC = row counter reading
rem = remain(ing)
rep = repeat
Rib G = rib gauge
RT = right
sc = single crochet
sl = slip
str = straight
st(s) = stitch(es)
st st = stockinette stitch
TD = tension or stitch size dial
tog = together
trans = transfer
UWP = upper working position
WP = working position
WY = waste yarn
yb = yarn back (handknitting term)
yfwd = yarn forward
(handknitting term)

CASTING ON

The edges of the fabric are an important finishing detail. In the manual for your machine, you will have instructions on how to cast on, but here are some good methods, which may not be in your manual, but which can be done on any make of machine. They are not necessarily advanced techniques – they offer you alternatives.

HAND CAST ON

You can experiment with edges and cast on or bind off in such a way that the edge becomes a special detail. If you don't have a ribber on your machine, create a rib with a hand-texture technique or handknit the ribs. Casting on by hand produces a firm knitted edge which is good enough to use on its own as the hem of a garment. It is also known as an e-wrap cast on.

Select the number of needles required to HP, with the carriage on the right hand side, and set the machine to knit. Thread the yarn through the antenna, and starting from the left side, make a loose knot around the first needle on the left (1). Now wind the yarn counter-clockwise around all the needles (2), maintaining an even tension and making sure the loops are kept well back towards the machine. Thread the yarn through the main feeder and knit 1 row. Check that all the cast-on stitches have been knitted. Push the work well down (return needles to HP), and knit 2 more rows in this way. Hang on weights or a comb when your work measures about 2.5cm (1in).

FOOLPROOF CAST ON

This is not only for beginners, it is also a good way for knitters to join pieces of knitting together. Take a swatch of knitted fabric, even the sleeve of an old sweater, and hook any firm part of the fabric onto the needles (don't try to pick up an unraveled edge of stitching), taking one loop to one needle (3). You can use a transfer tool or do this by hand. Make sure that the loops are not too bulky for the machine to take. Set the carriage to knit, bring the needles to HP and knit 1 row on a loose gauge.

It is better to work the first row in a slippery nylon or rayon cord so that it can be removed easily. Change to waste yarn and work 2-3cm (1-1½in) before removing the rayon thread. Hang on weights or a comb.

It is always a good idea to use rayon thread to separate knitted sections of fabric. (Any easily removable thread such as nylon is appropriate.) This is known as a drawthread. When it is removed, the pieces of knitting will be separated from each other.

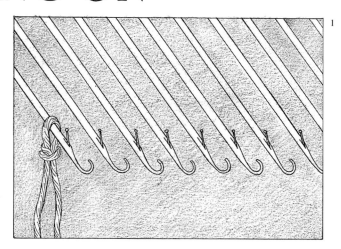

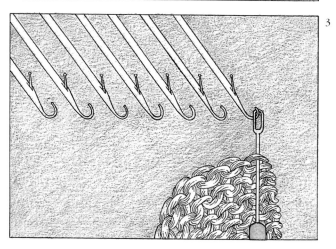

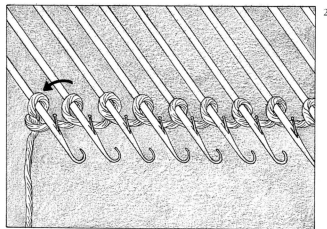

CLOSED EDGE CAST ON

This edge is a quick way of making a secure cast on that will not unravel. It is suitable for sampling. If you want a firmer edge, or if you want to turn up a welt, it is better to cast on with waste yarn.

Bring all the needles to be cast on forward to WP, then bring every other needle to HP (4). Set the machine to hold and work 1 row (white yarn in 5). Set machine to knit and work 1 row (pink yarn in 5). The cast on is then complete.

LADDER STOP

When casting on, double-bed knitters should always work a ladder stop before they begin a rib. If you compare the edges on commercial knitwear with those of domestic knitting, you will notice how neat and firm the manufactured edge is. It is the attention to detail that produces good edges and a simple structure like the ladder stop does make all the difference.

Ladder stop (6) is a technique much used in industry because it is then easy to separate the waste yarn from the garment and to achieve a better edge.

Cast on both beds with waste yarn (I have used two contrast yarns to show the technique more clearly), work about 5cm (2in) on all needles, then work as follows. Work 3 rows on back bed, 1 row on both beds. Work 3 rows on front bed, 1 row on both beds. Take carriage across without yarn, selecting to knit on front bed and selecting non-knit on back bed. The stitches on the front bed will drop off and now the machine is ready for you to work the welt in the correct yarn.

When the work is finished, remove the slack thread (cream) which has formed a zigzag, and your work will be easily separated from the waste yarn.

This structure is useful if you want to go from working on two beds to working on one without removing the work from the machine. To end up working on the front bed only, repeat the structure as before but starting on the front bed and finishing by dropping the stitches off the back bed.

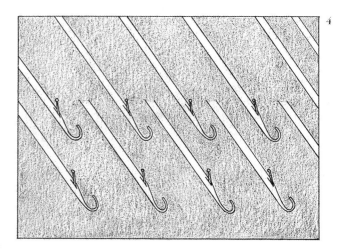
4

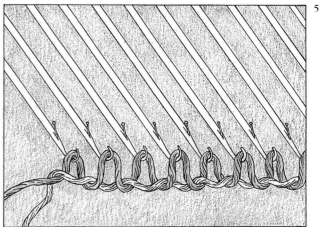
5

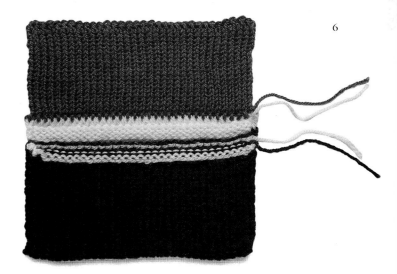
6

BINDING OFF

The most common means of binding off on a knitting machine is the single transfer tool bind off. However, depending on the reason for binding off, you can choose a number of other ways to bind off. The bind off edge may be a feature of your garment, on a neckline welt for example, but even if it is not, it must be gauged correctly so that it is neither too loose nor too tight.

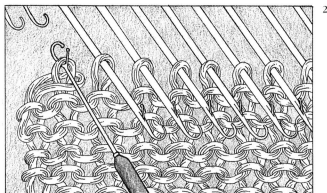

AROUND GATE PEGS BIND OFF

This method of binding off around the gate pegs is similar to the regular bind off edge, but it holds the bind off edge on the machine so that the work is evenly stretched until binding off is complete. The method is the same as for the regular bind off using a single transfer tool.

Slip the stitch onto the gate peg as you slip it onto the needle – the stitch slips over the gate peg and needle at the same time (1). Proceed as for the normal bind off edge, but slipping every stitch onto the gate peg each time. This keeps the work hanging on the machine. When the bind off is complete, lift the work off the machine.

If you don't have gate pegs, place the bind off chain back onto the machine at about 5-needle intervals to hold the edge straight.

Another version of this bind off is to take the stitch around the back of the gate peg and onto the needle. This is faster and easier, making a less raised chain.

LATCH TOOL BIND OFF

This bind off method uses a latch tool (you could substitute a machine needle). This produces a more defined edge especially when binding off two edges together. The row before the bind off is worked at a looser gauge; therefore this method is more suitable for a bind off row, not for decreasing over a limited area.

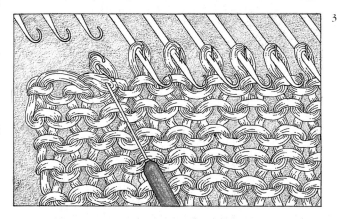

Bring all the needles forward to HP and slip the latch tool through the first stitch at the opposite end to the carriage and yarn end. Take the stitch behind the latch of the tool, push back the needle, and take the second stitch into the hook of the tool. Pull the tool so the first stitch slips off and the second is left in the hook of the tool (2). Repeat this process along the row (3).

To bind off the last stitch, pull the yarn end through it with the latch tool (4). This method is rather like crocheting an edge. Hold the work firmly as you go to maintain a good tension. The width of your bind off edge must correspond to the width of your garment. The advantages of this technique are that the knitter is in full control of the tension, and the bind off can be worked after the knitting has been removed from the machine onto waste yarn.

BINDING OFF TOGETHER

This is a good method of joining a garment together. It can be worked with right or wrong sides together, depending on whether you want the bind off chain to be visible or not. This method greatly reduces the amount of hand work you have to do, making finishing quicker because you are doing it as you go along. To prepare the different garment sections for this bind off, the earlier knitted sections should be bound off on waste yarn so that they can be hooked on later, the waste yarn unraveled and the seam bound off.

Hook the first edge of the work onto the machine with the right side facing you unless you want the chain bind off edge on the right side, in which case hook up with the wrong side facing you. (You can bind off together at the end of knitting without taking the garment section off the machine.) Pick up every stitch on a shoulder seam, but if you are working on side seams, pick up the big loops formed by every other row (5). Hook the second section to be joined over the first in the same way and bring the needles into HP. Knit 1 row. This should be at a looser gauge if the fabric is bulky or if a thicker end is being used to accentuate the bind off edge. Bind off to release from machine.

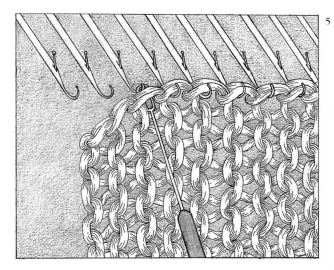

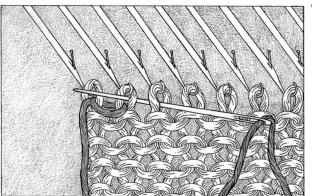

TWO BED BIND OFF

To bind off on a double bed machine, transfer all the needles to the back bed so that you have two stitches on each needle on the back bed. If you are working on a structure in which needles are left out, this will obviously result in some needles only having one stitch on them. That will not affect the bind off. I find a double-eyed bodkin is invaluable for this kind of transfer (page 140). Knit 1 row. Bind off as usual.

TAPESTRY NEEDLE BIND OFF

This method of binding off can be used for a complete row or for small decreases. It is similar to backstitch. Thread the yarn end through a tapestry needle and working from the left side of the work, insert the needle into the front of the first stitch, then through from the front of the second stitch and out through the back of the first stitch. Put the needle into the front of the third stitch (6) and back out through the second stitch and so on to the end of the row or required number of stitches.

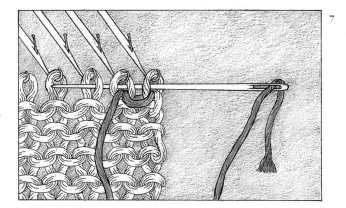

If you are working from the right, start in the same way securing the first and second stitches, but for the next stitch, cross behind the second stitch, skipping it, and coming back through the third stitch (7).

If you bind off two edges together, or one edge, such as a collar or rib, onto a finished edge, this is known as handlinking. If done neatly, it looks very professional.

WELTS & RIBS

The welts and ribs of a garment need to be neat and worked on the correct gauge so that they do not distort with the stretching of wearing and washing. A rib structure (whether 1 × 1 or 2 × 1) is one of the most common and efficient edges for waists, sleeves and necklines. If you have a double bed machine, this is easily produced. If not, you can either hand tool or handknit your rib. If you plan to handknit your rib and hang it onto the machine, first check that the rib is the right gauge by making a small sample and hooking it onto the machine.

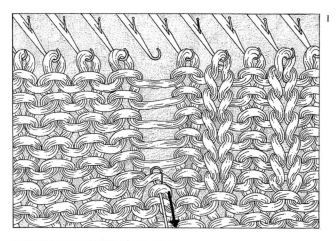

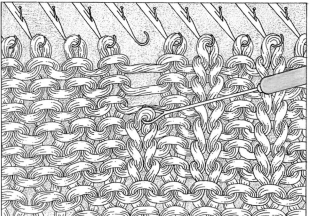

MAKING A WELT

A welt is simple to knit and can be finished on the machine. Cast on the required number of sts, work for about 10 rows in WY, alter the gauge at least one size tighter than the main gauge for the garment (do a sample for this). Work the depth of the welt in the MY. loosen the gauge by 2 sizes, K 1 R. Return to the welt gauge and K the row for the welt depth again. Pick up the first MY row st for st (1), unravel the WY, check that all the needles carry 2 sts, and that all sts are caught, change to the main gauge and cont with the knitting. The loose turning row can be worked tighter than this (page 72).

HAND TOOLED RIB

This is the method for making a rib on a single bed machine, using a latch tool. It is somewhat time-consuming, but worth the effort.

To make a K1 P1 rib, cast on and work 2.5cm (1in) plain knitting, then leaving the first 1 st, drop 1 st to form a ladder (1) and latch it back up from the side facing you (2), thus forming a rib of 1 K st on the wrong side of the work showing as 1 P st on the right side of the work. Repeat this across the width of the fabric.

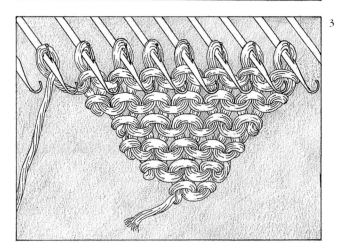

POINTED EDGE

Points are often used for edgings by handknitters and they go well with lace fabrics. Set the machine to knit and thread your chosen yarn. On the right of the machine, at least 8 needles from the end, cast on one stitch using the hand cast-on method. It is advisable to use a small weight such as a key or washer for this type of edge.

Working 1 R over 1 st as directed, with the carr at the LT side, cast on 1 more st to the RT of the first. Then form another st to the LT of the first st. You now have 3 sts and have worked 3 R. Rep this procedure until you have 15 sts. K 1 R. Bring the carr to the LT side.

Bring all the N to HP, unthread the yarn, break off enough to hold the sts and sew in later, and set the machine to hold. Select the 8th N to the LT of the work – count the first empty N to the LT as first – and rep the procedure to form a 2nd point (3). When you have formed the required number of points, work 1 R to join all the points together.

When working the second and following points, make sure the "made" stitches are in the WP. If you have difficulty, you can put each point onto WY and rehang them when they have all been knitted. Alternatively you can put the sts into the hook of the needle with the latch tool (page 120) to prevent the needles which should be knitting from shooting into HP.

TUCKED RIB

This is another rib effect, which has textured detail caused by tuck stitches (4). This type of rib can be used on plain or textured garments to add interest.

Cast on an odd number of sts in K1 P1 arrangement. Trans sts to back bed to make 3 sts on back bed and 2 sts on front bed. TD 7, set machine to hold, push center N of sets of 3 sts on back bed to HP. K 3 R. Set machine to knit back from HP. K 1 R. Cont in this patt until required depth of rib. This fabric looks interesting from both sides, so is effectively reversible.

CABLED RIB

The cabled rib looks most effective when it is used on a garment that already has cables incorporated into it.

Cast on an odd number of sts in a K1 P1 arrangement. Trans sts to back bed to make 4 sts on back bed and 3 sts on front bed. TD 7, work cable over sets of 4 sts on back bed ev 4th R. Cont until required depth of rib (5).

TWO-COLOR FAIR ISLE WELT

This welt can be done with a punchcard 2 stopped and setting the machine for single bed Fair Isle (page 119) or with hand selection. It can be made to look like a rib (6), with the floats at the back of the fabric helping to restrict width.

Cast on sts using the e-wrap method. TD 8, using the MY for the 1st 2 sts and CY for the next 2 sts and so on all along the R. Cont working 2 sts MY and 2 sts CY until the required depth of the welt is knitted. Change to TD 7 and K st st or your chosen fabric.

INCREASING & DECREASING

WALE DEFLECTION INCREASE

Increasing and decreasing is simple on a machine, but you have to decide on the method if you want to use the shaping technique to create an effect. Wale deflection (similar in some ways to fully fashioned) is a detail used on many commercially knitted garments. The technique gives a good edge, and creates a chevron effect with the wales of the stitches. Shapings can tighten the edges, especially if worked over the end stitches. Fashioning several stitches, therefore, not only produces a nice detail, but leaves the end stitch undisturbed to give a neater seam.

This increase can be worked over any number of stitches. It is shown here worked with 2 stitches. Using a 2-prong transfer tool, pick up the edge 2 stitches and move them out one position, leaving the third needle from the end empty (1). Fill the empty needle with a stitch formed by the last row on the next needle – the fourth stitch on the last row (2). This would work using the loop taken from the second stitch to the right as well.

If you want to work the wale deflection detail up a straight edge, you have to increase or decrease depending on which way you want the chevrons to slant. Increases slant outwards, decreases inwards. You must allow for the stitch lost or gained.

WALE DEFLECTION DECREASE

To make a wale deflection decrease, with a 3-prong transfer tool, pick up the edge three stitches and move them one position inwards, leaving the end needle empty (3). If you wish to work straight, bring this needle forward to HP and work the next row normally. The needle will pick up the loop (4).

If you wish to shape in the middle of the fabric, a waist or bust dart for example, fashion in the normal way and move all the stitches either in or out, depending on whether you are increasing or decreasing, one position. This is more time-consuming, but gives the advantage of a properly fitted garment with nice details.

Wale deflection can also be used as a detail in the center of the work. An example of this is the front panel on the basic shirt (page 72). It is important to be careful how frequently you transfer relatively large numbers of stitches. Done too often, it will twist and distort the fabric.

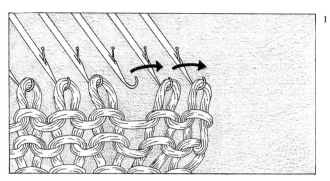

1

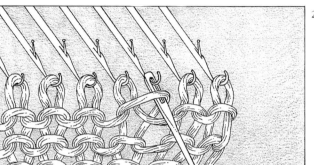

2

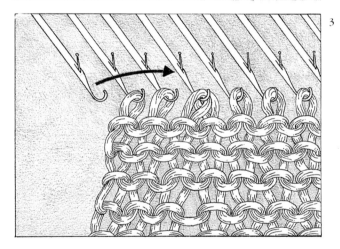

3

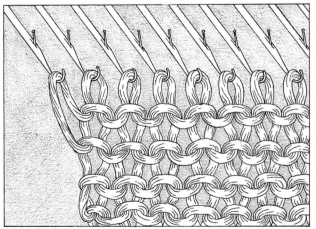

4

EDGES

Attention to detail is all part of the development of the design and makes a lot of difference to the finished article. You will notice when making knitwear that often the garment can look disastrous until the last seam is finished, or the neck rib or welt is added. The trims and edges act as a frame for the finished article and they must be considered as an integral part of the design of the garment. Without them the design may not "work."

CABLE EDGE

The cable edge pattern is written for double bed machines but single-bed knitters can form the detail using hand texture (page 32). Although the cable is shown on a decreased edge, it is also effective when worked up straight edges, such as on armholes and side seams. It is advisable when working such an edge to add a couple of extra stitches for the seam.

To form a cable, take 2 stitches onto a tool in your left hand and rest the tool on the gate pegs out of the way to the left of the empty needles. Holding the first 2 stitches in the tool in your left hand, pick up the next 2 stitches to the right with a tool in your right hand and place them on the empty needles on the far left (the first 2 that were emptied). Now take the stitches in your left hand and put them onto the 2 empty needles on the right side. This completes the cable.

To make the cable edge (1), cast on 33 stitches in a K1 P1 rib arrangement. Transfer all the stitches to the front bed except for the 2 edge stitches and the 6th stitch in from each edge. TD 7. Work the cable over the 2 sets of 4 stitches between the 2 purl stitches on every 4th row. At the same time, decrease 1 stitch on every 4th row on the 7th stitch in from each end. Move the stitch along both beds as the decreases are worked. Continue until row 50.

PURL EDGE

Working the reverse stitch for a seam detail is a technique often used in handknitting and commercial knitwear. The purl edge (2) shows a plain purl edging. Using hand texture, the purl areas could be worked in moss stitch or even seeded rib (page 32).

Remember when working out how many stitches to use in this detail that the area will be doubled when seams are joined. Also allow for stitches to be taken into seams during making up.

Cast on 33 stitches in a K1 P1 rib arrangement. Transfer all stitches to the front bed except for stitches 3, 4 and 5 in from each end. TD 7. Decrease 1 stitch on every 4th row on the 6th stitch in from each end. Move stitches along both beds as the decreases are worked. Continue until row 50.

1

2

FINISHING

There are endless examples, views and opinions on good finishing for knitwear. For me the best is the most logical solution with most esthetic result. This need not be the most complicated. The best education any student of knitwear design can obtain regarding finish (other than that of direct commercial experience) is to look at existing merchandise. Look at different price levels. You will be amazed at the professionalism that can be easily copied with domestic resources, and appalled at the quality of many "commercial" attempts.

Throughout this book and especially in the collection, I have encouraged the use of grafting together on the machine; it not only forms an interesting seam, but it makes a join that will stretch with the fabric. The other advantage is that the garment is far nearer to completion when leaving the machine. Many subtle design features can be incorporated into the joining and finishing of a garment; it is important to gain inspiration from traditional handknit work. Look at Norwegian or Scottish work and you will see that they don't just treat the ribs

and collars as additions; they integrate the whole piece of work, and this can easily be done with machine work, though it seldom is!

The finish of a garment refers to the way it is put together, the trims that are chosen and how they are attached, the way edges and other similar details are dealt with and the blocking and pressing. Many points on finishing have been covered in other parts of this book, such as hooking on and seaming on the machine. The important thing to remember is to try and join the garment and add trims and details as neatly and practically as possible.

It is essential to work neatly if you want a professional-looking garment. The edges of the work must be straight with no loops and baggy stitches. If you are working with small balls of yarn, try and make the ball finish where the end can easily be hidden.

If you make a mistake, unravel the rows that are wrong and reknit. You can put on an unraveling accessory.

HAND SEWING

Hand sewing is a perfect method for joining all seams on a garment, especially pocket welts and ribs which need matching exactly. I find hand finishing garments is sometimes quicker than complex machine finishing.

I prefer to work from the right side of the fabric and pick up the same amount of rows from each piece. Setting in sleeves by hand means the sleeve cap can be eased into place accurately.

Mattress stitch is an almost invisible seam. Place the two pieces to be joined next to each other on a flat surface with right sides facing you, insert the tapestry needle through the two bar loops next to the selvedge stitch (1). Take the needle to the other side and pick up two bar loops on that side. Pull the yarn tight every few rows. Continue working this way for the whole seam. The selvedge will be hidden when the yarn is pulled tight. This method of seaming can also be used to make a flat seam (2, purl side shown).

Overstitching creates a slight ridge on the outside of the seam. Place together the wrong sides of the pieces to be joined. With the threaded tapestry needle, pick up the outside of the bound off stitch on one piece and take the needle to the other side (3). Work from side to side until the seam is completed. This must be done neatly if it is to look good. Take the same loop of each stitch every time.

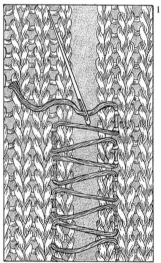

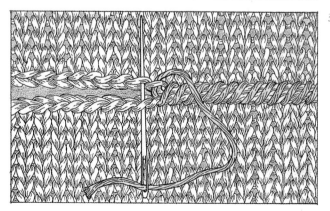

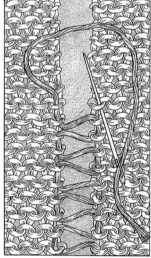

CROCHET EDGES

Crochet stitches are a neat way to finish an edge or to join a seam.

To do a slip stitch edge, hold the work with the right side facing you, secure the yarn and insert the crochet hook through the stitch. Catch the yarn and pull it through the first stitch. Insert the hook through the next stitch, yarn around hook, pull it through the stitch and through the loop on the hook (4). The intervals between the stitches you pick up has to be carefully considered so that the edge is neither puckered nor too loose.

A single crochet edge is slightly bulkier than the slip stitch edge (page 38). Commence as for the slip stitch edge, but bring the yarn through the loop again (5). Insert the hook into the next stitch, wind the yarn around the hook and draw it through the loop, then take yarn around the hook (6) and draw it through both loops on the crochet hook.

To make a picot edge, work 1 sc and then ∗ make 4 chains. Join the first ch to the last ch with a sl st. This forms a tiny loop. 1 sc into next st on the main fabric. Rep from ∗ to ∗ along the edge.

LINKING

This is a process used commercially for joining fabrics. The trims are knitted onto waste yarn, then the edge of the trim is joined to the garment by picking up each loop, and slipping it onto a metal point on a linking machine. The edge of the garment is also placed on the point and both are joined with a chain stitch automatically made by the linker. This can be done by hand (see tapestry needle bind off, page 123).

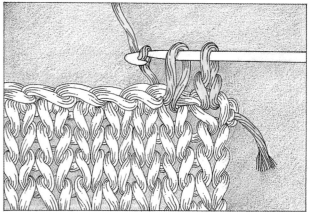

This method of joining produces neat seams and stitches can be linked off to form a fine finished edge. Knitters should allow for linking in the structure and design of their trims by knitting the row to be linked a point or two looser so that it is easy to put onto the machine and there is room to form the chain stitch.

Double bed knitters can make a linking slot. This is done by working about 1cm (½in) of tubular knitting on the end of a collar or placket and putting it onto waste yarn, still in tubular. The edge of the garment can then be sandwiched into the tubular and linked into place. Domestic linkers are easy to work and provide good finishes. You can also link by hand in the same way, by using backstitch.

SERGING/OVERLOCKING

Serging or overlocking is a stitch which secures raw edges. It is universal for knitted fabrics, but care must be taken to achieve a neat result. The machine actually cuts the edge of the fabric and works a stitch around it using 3 or 4 threads. The 4-thread type is the best for knitwear. It is more reliable, neat and more secure but is used mostly in industry. The 3-thread type is perfectly adequate for domestic needs and easier to find. Some sergers have differential feed to avoid puckering knit fabrics. Serging is normally used for cut-and-sew knitwear – garments which are actually cut out of a piece of knitted fabric and sewn together.

There are other joining methods used commercially, but the machinery is complex and not as readily available or affordable to the home knitter.

SWISS DARNING

Swiss darning is a type of embroidery usually associated with handknitting, but it can also be applied on machine knitting. It covers the machine-knitted stockinette stitches exactly to give the illusion that the color has been knitted in.

It is useful for disguising mistakes and can be time-saving, especially when working a complex intarsia when some of the finer detail can be added after knitting. It also saves using too many colors in a row at the time of knitting. The fine lines on the Argyle design (7) were Swiss darned. It can be used for motifs or monograms, or to add more color to Fair Isle.

Using a contrast yarn similar in thickness to the main yarn (but not thinner than it), begin at the bottom of the line to be darned, bringing the needle through the base of the first stitch. Insert the needle from right to left behind the stitch above (8). Take it to the back of the fabric through the base of the original stitch (9). If you are working horizontally, bring the needle back to the front through the base of the next stitch to the left, or if working vertically, through the base of the stitch above.

When Swiss darning, work with a tapestry needle. The blunt end will not split the yarn of the stitches. Work one color at a time, and secure the yarn properly at the beginning and end of the darning.

If you are working over a large area, work horizontally across the rows to give a denser covering. If the design misses a few stitches or rows, leave a float across the back of the work. Make sure you don't pull the yarn too tight or leave it too loose.

If you are designing your own Swiss-darned motifs, work them out first on stitch-related graph paper so you can see how they will look when finished.

7

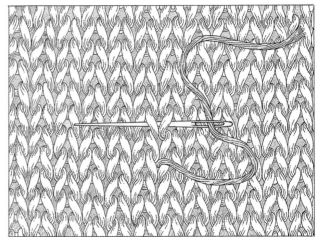

8

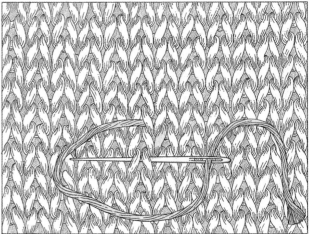

9

BLOCKING

Blocking is used to arrange the pieces of a garment so that they conform to the shape and dimensions in the measurement diagram. This can either be done before they are sewn together, or when the pieces are taken off the machine with the shoulder joined.

Use a blanket or thick towel and arrange the garment in the correct shape, securing the edges with pins. Place the pins at frequent intervals so that you do not ripple the seams. Pin them as you would a sewing pattern to fabric to keep the edges straight (10).

Dampen the fabric either by directing steam over it, or spray water over it and leave it to dry. Always refer to the manufacturer's instructions, never push an iron across knitting and do not block a ribbed fabric. Synthetic fibers should be treated with caution.

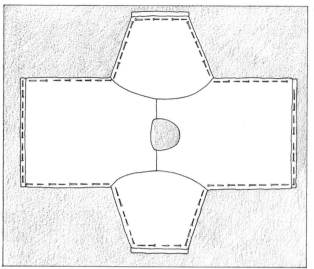

10

PRESSING

Pressing makes all the difference to the finished knitwear. You need to use plenty of steam. Domestic irons with an extra steam facility are quite adequate. You could get by with a hot iron and a wet cloth. Be careful with raised patterns such as cables, and tucks. It is better to block them, steam them or spray with water and leave to dry without any pressing.

Be sure to keep your iron set warm enough to have an effect, but cool enough not to singe the fabric. Start with the side seam. Blow steam at it and pat it with your fingers. Work up the underarm seam and lightly press the shoulder seams and sleeve cap. Next straighten the garment and press the front and back armhole flat; do both sides, then the neck. Lay the garment out flat with the shoulder folded at the seam, then carefully steam the neckline. Don't pull ribs because you will take all the elasticity out of them.

If you do overpress a garment, you may be able to salvage it by washing. It may be necessary to run elastic through saggy ribs but sometimes, especially with wool, they bounce back with a blow of steam. Synthetic fibers are more likely to pose a problem if overpressed, so exercise caution.

WASHING

Try to keep the work in progress as clean as possible. Put your cones on a clean surface or paper and keep your machine free from too much oil. Many yarns benefit from washing before knitting but some never look quite the same again, so aim to have to wash (wet finish) your work out of choice rather than necessity. Yarns, especially pale-colored yarns, should be kept in polythene bags to help with this problem. Knitting rooms do get very dusty. Some fibers have to be washed before wear because they still have natural oils in them or feel rough to the touch.

Garments knitted in lambswool and similar fibers tend to shrink and soften after washing, whereas Shetland does not usually shrink. Follow the instructions on the ball/cone band and be careful with spinning and tumble drying. Don't think that a slightly different wash method will be all right; hand washing is the best solution unless you have a machine with a gentle hand wash cycle. Wash your work after sewing it together; this will help to hide any imperfections.

DRYING

Knitted garments are better dried flat, but if the fabric is quite a tight knit, put it on the line; it probably will not drop. It is best to dry in fresh air – be very careful with tumble dryers. The denim skirts (page 69) were shrunk in a tumble dryer but this was a carefully controlled exercise; try to use these machines to your advantage.

BRUSHING

Brushing may be used to emphasize the characteristic of a yarn which tends to fluff up, such as mohair. If a fabric of two or more colors is brushed it will give the illusion of blending to create a new color. Plain wools will not give such an interesting effect.

CHARTS

INTARSIA page 44

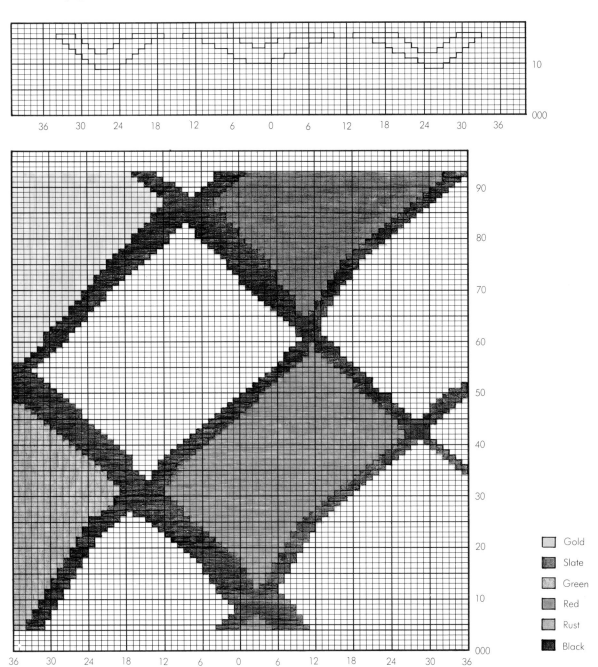

Gold
Slate
Green
Red
Rust
Black

LACE page 36

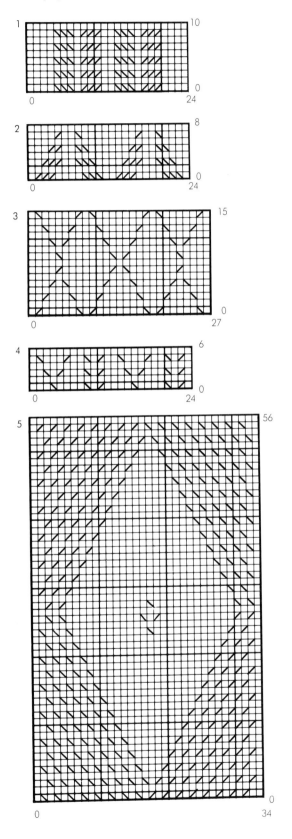

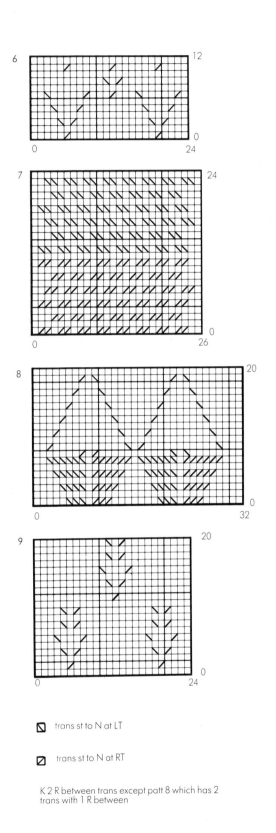

◩ trans st to N at LT

◪ trans st to N at RT

K 2 R between trans except patt 8 which has 2
trans with 1 R between

HAND TEXTURE page 32

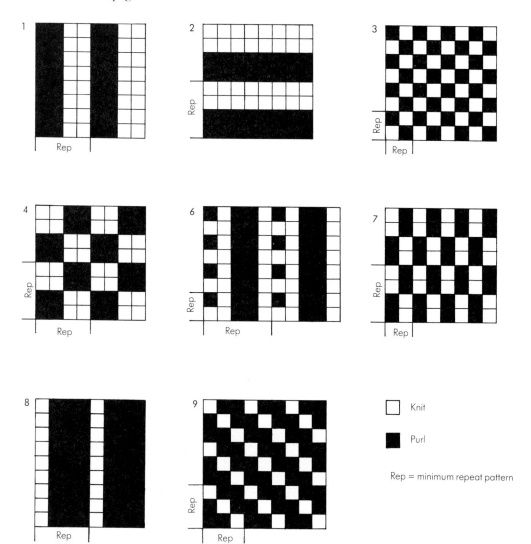

	Knit
■	Purl

Rep = minimum repeat pattern

Stitch-related graph paper can be bought in large sheets, but if you cannot find any in the shops, use this grid (opposite) by photocopying it and taping several sheets together. It will be easier to use if you enlarge it. The grid relates to the width of the stitch, so you can draw a design that will not be distorted when it is knitted.

PUNCHCARDS

Punchcards provide an automatic needle selection for use in conjunction with the different functions of the machine. The needles are selected and the technique interprets the pattern in its own way. Singer/Studio card 1 is used throughout this book, and it illustrates the point perfectly. In the Fair Isle section (page 26) it produces spots and selecting on every other needle (fabrics 7, 3) and in the tuck section (page 30), it produces a tuck on every other needle (fabric 6).

Not all cards are interchangeable to all techniques. For example, tuck cards have one knit stitch between each tucked stitch; tucking over consecutive needles when working on one bed would produce large loops which would jam the machine (an exception is fabric 3 and 9 on page 30). A card selecting several needles in succession used with slip stitch would form loops which would not interfere with the work (fabric 5, page 38).

Your machine manual will indicate which cards can be used for which techniques and it is a good idea to try out these cards to see exactly what restrictions there are and how different techniques work with the same card.

Different machines read cards in different ways; some machines select the holes punched, others select the unpunched squares. Some machines bring pre-selected needles to UWP (these are known as pre-selecting machines); some pattern the needles in WP. Repeats also vary. The most popular standard repeat is 24, but there are also 8, 12, 24, 40, 60, and up to 200 repeats available. New machines offer the knitter much more, but you must work within the repeat of your machine, unless you wish to hand select. This is obviously more time-consuming as you are doing the job of the card, telling the machine which needles to use and when. This type of work does, however, teach you how to re-position the needles when working with a card, should the knitting fall off.

When designing your own punchcards you must be sure that you are working with a number of stitches that multiply exactly into your repeat. If you are working on a small repeat, it is a good idea to isolate a multiple of squares on graph paper so that you are sure to work exactly within your repeat. Larger, more figurative designs are also better worked on graph paper beforehand, but work on the center of the design first so that you can make the edges of the design fit together.

It is important to consider where you would like the pattern to be placed on the work and single-motif facilities are provided on most modern machinery. This enables one repeat of the design to be isolated and positioned in any place across the knitting. This facility is more versatile on some machines than others. If you own a machine which does not have an automatic pattern isolation facility but pre-selects the needle to UWP, then simply push back (to WP) the needles that you do not want to select and you will only pattern on the needles you leave out. Owners of non-pre-selecting machines would have to bring forward needles not to be selected to HP which is a little more time-consuming.

The machine reads from your punchcard in reverse, so if you are working on a design that will only work one way, such as lettering, punch from the wrong side of your card and feed it into your machine with the right side facing.

Machines do not read the row you see above the machine (as it appears). They read several rows down. To find out how many rows a machine reads, insert the card with the first row level with the machine, take the carriage across and count how many rows you must knit before your first row selects.

You can stop your card so that it selects the same needles each row for vertical stripes, tuck, slip or weave patterns. It is also possible to elongate the pattern by selecting each row twice. These facilities can be worked out from your manual or from the function list on page 119.

Notations appear on cards and manuals explain all their uses. These can be confusing for the novice and it is quite possible to work without them with the exception of those used with the lace carriage. It is better to get into the habit of knowing exactly where you are, color and patternwise, within your knitting in case you have any problems such as the card jamming or work falling off the machine. This way you will be able to reset the machine or the punchcard and continue working.

It is important to learn to play with your machine so that you can find out what it can do. A domestic machine is not that fragile, so don't be afraid of damaging it, but never force the machine.

It is always advisable to mark the holes to be punched on your card before you make the holes. You can then check that you have it correctly marked out. Cover any mistakes with adhesive tape.

For many of the fabrics in this book I have used Singer/Studio punchcards 1, 2, 3, 7, and 8, and they are reproduced opposite. The Fair Isle punchcards are used on the sampler on page 27.

If your machine takes 60-stitch repeat punchcards then you will have to adapt the cards. For Singer/Studio punchcards 1, 2, 3 and 7 repeat 20 stitches three times. For Fair Isle punchcards 4, 5, 6 and 7 repeat 20 stitches (of the 40-stitch repeat) three times. For patterns that will not repeat to 60 stitches (Singer/Studio punchcard 8 and Fair Isle punchcard 3) you will have to adapt the pattern, making sure that the edges will work together.

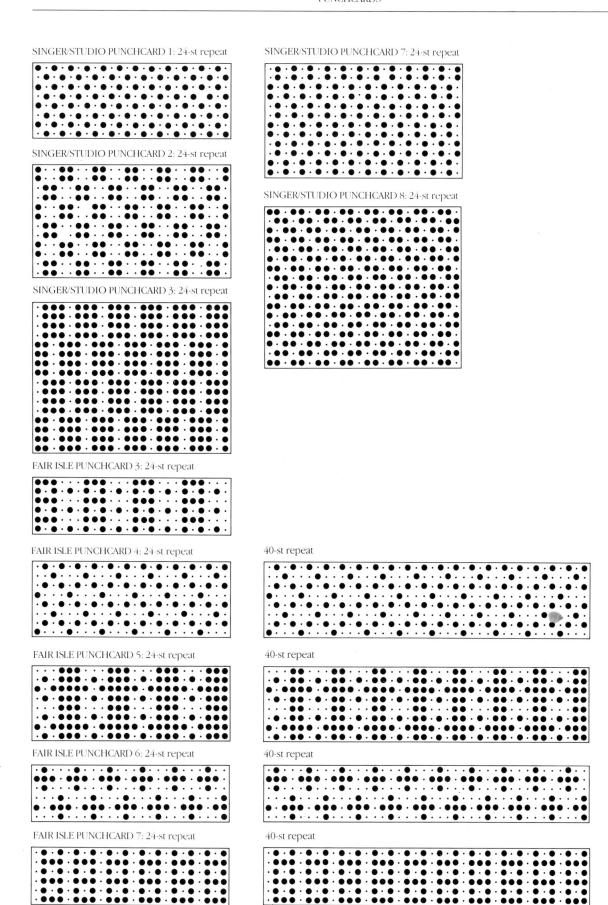

SINGER/STUDIO PUNCHCARD 1: 24-st repeat

SINGER/STUDIO PUNCHCARD 2: 24-st repeat

SINGER/STUDIO PUNCHCARD 3: 24-st repeat

FAIR ISLE PUNCHCARD 3: 24-st repeat

FAIR ISLE PUNCHCARD 4: 24-st repeat

FAIR ISLE PUNCHCARD 5: 24-st repeat

FAIR ISLE PUNCHCARD 6: 24-st repeat

FAIR ISLE PUNCHCARD 7: 24-st repeat

SINGER/STUDIO PUNCHCARD 7: 24-st repeat

SINGER/STUDIO PUNCHCARD 8: 24-st repeat

40-st repeat

40-st repeat

40-st repeat

40-st repeat

GLOSSARY

antenna – a spring attached to the upper tension mast through which the yarn must be threaded on its way to the carriage. It regulates the flow of yarn to the correct tension. Also known as a mast, yarn break, upper tension unit.

blocking – laying out a garment to the finished measurements and steaming it to fix the shape.

Botany wool – wool from Australian merino sheep.

bouclé – a textured yarn with tiny loops along its surface at irregular intervals.

cable – stitches crossed over to create a braid-like effect; any number of stitches can be involved.

cams – tracks under the carriage which, when set by the levers on the carriage, put the needles in the required positions for type of knitting.

carriage – the piece of the machine that moves across the stitches to knit them. On some machines carriages have function buttons or levers to select different stitches automatically, such as tuck, knitweave etc. Also contains the tension or stitch dial. A double bed machine has two carriages which are coupled during double bed knitting.

casting-on comb – a heavy bar which holds down the fabric when knitting (see page 140).

charting devices – see accessories (page 140).

chenille – a textured yarn like velvet.

circular knitting – also known as tubular, this is possible on a double bed machine when the carriage knits across one bed and back along the other, knitting in the round.

color changer – see accessories (page 140).

count number – a system of measuring yarn thickness.

cut-and-sew – after a length of fabric is knitted straight, the shape is cut out and the edges sewn and serged as in dressmaking.

double bed jacquard – a method of producing color patterns. The yarns not in use are worked in a stripe or birdseye pattern on the reverse side of the fabric.

end – one strand of yarn.

e-wrap – hand cast on method to produce a good edge in which the yarn is wrapped around the needles by hand.

face side – the knit side of the fabric.

Fair Isle – originally traditional knitting from the Scottish Islands; it has floats on the reverse side.

floats – yarn that passes over knitting to the next worked stitch. In industry usually jumps no more than 6 stitches at one time.

free move (FM) – set the machine not to knit, so the carriage can pass over the needles without knitting them. Also known as non-knit.

front bed – the bed nearest the knitter on a double bed machine; the ribber.

full pitch – on a double bed machine, when the needles on both sides are exactly opposite each other.

fully fashioned – decorative method of knitting to shape where the decreases or increases will show on the right side of the fabric.

gansey – traditional fisherman's sweater, closely knitted in fine worsted wool, usually in the round. Patterns vary according to the area and are often associated with families or villages.

gate pegs – pins which run along the front of the needle bed. Also known as sinker posts.

gauge (tension) – the number of rows and stitches in a given yarn, over a given measurement – usually 10cm (4in) square, needed to produce the requisite measurements so that the garment will knit up to the size given on the measurement diagram. Also the number of needles every 2.5cm (1in). Standard machines have 200 needles and are 6 gauge; bulky machines are a heavier gauge.

godet – triangular-shaped panel, often in a skirt.

grafting – joining two raw edges together by hand by filling in a row.

half pitch – on a double bed machine, when the needles on one bed are opposite the gate pegs on the other bed.

hand selection – selecting needles by hand.

hand-wound twister – see accessories page 140.

hank – yarn wound in a large loop.

holding – also known as partial knitting in which some of the needles are put out of work (HP), usually for shaping, color work, or when one part of the fabric is held while the other part is being knitted.

holding position (HP) – needles are held out of action.

intarsia – color patterns where the yarn is laid over the needles by hand and there are no floats across the back of the work.

inlay – see knitweave.

knitweave – a setting on the machine which enables you to weave in yarns.

ladder – a vertical line in the knitting made up of short horizontal floats produced when a stitch has unraveled or the needles have been left in NWP.

latch tool (hook) – tool similar to machine knitting needle but with a plastic handle, used to pick up dropped stitches or to bind off an edge by hand.

locked – when a punchcard is stopped on a row in order to knit that row twice (see stopped).

main bed – also known as the back bed.

main feed(er) – the yarn is fed through this feeder. The second feeder takes the contrast yarn in Fair Isle knitting.

marl – a yarn produced when yarns are twisted together.

mattress stitch – method of hand seaming on knitted fabric (page 128).

moss stitch – K1, P1 on one row, P1, K1 on the next row, over an even number of stitches making a textured fabric.

needle – holds the stitches on the machine, parts consist of the hook, the latch, stem, butt and shank (page 119).

needle positions or set-out – see page 119.

needle selections – depending on the sophistication of your machine, selection can be made manually with a selector comb, by pressing buttons, or by using a punchcard. Those needles not selected remain in working position (WP) on some machines and move forward to UWP on others.

non-working position (NWP) – needles in this position remain out of action.

nylon cord – sometimes called a drawthread or ravel cord, this is knitted after waste yarn has been knitted but before the main yarn is started so that when the knitting is finished, the waste yarn can be easily separated from the main fabric by pulling out the slippery cord.

partial knitting – short-row knitting, or using holding technique.

placket – faced opening to take a zipper or buttons.

plaid – a check or tartan type of design.

presser-foot – a gadget on the carriage which holds down the work, making it possible to knit without a comb or weights.

punchcards – plastic cards with holes punched to produce a needle selection to be used in conjunction with techniques.

purl stitch – on a single bed machine, a stitch made from reverse side of knitting; it is a back loop. A knit stitch is a face loop.

racking – on a double bed machine, moving the ribber or front bed to the right or left in multiples of needle positions, usually by means of a lever.

reverse side – the side facing you during knitting, but, in fact, the purl side, or the wrong side of the fabric (unless you decide to use the fabric reversed).

ribber or ribbing attachment – an optional extra on a single bed machine, this is an extra needle bed that allows the knitter to make purl stitches on the right side of the fabric, thereby creating a rib.

row counter – shows the number of rows knitted. Patterns usually refer to RC 00.

sampling – testing ideas, yarns and stitches to find the correct combination for the design you want to make.

second bed – see ribber or front bed.

selector combs – also known as needle pushers, are used to select needles for ribs. Most are set, for example, 2 × 2. Some are changeable.

sheets – sheets of paper used on electronic machines to produce a needle selection. The design is drawn on the sheet. They have the same function as punchcards.

sideways knit – when a garment is knitted sideways, rather than from bottom to top.

single motif – isolated Fair Isle facility.

sinker – metal plate which is sprung and holds each stitch down so no weight is needed.

slip stitch – a setting on the machine where selected needles don't knit and the carriage passes over them creating raised "floats" on the reverse side of the fabric.

stitch dial – see tension dial.

stopped (a punchcard) – all rows are knitted with the same needle selection, expanding the uses of the punchcard.

swatch – a piece of knitting, usually used to check the gauge and to show different colorways and designs.

Swiss darning – hand embroidery over a knitted fabric to add color and detail to the design, or for mending and covering mistakes.

tension dial (TD) – a dial on the machine that changes the gauge or stitch size by tightening or loosening the yarn flow.

transfer – moving one or more stitches either from one needle to another on either side or across the beds on a double bed machine.

tuck – setting on the machine when yarn is laid over the needle onto the hook and knitted into a subsequent row. Tucking can be done several times on one needle, but the amount is limited.

upper working position (UWP) – a patterning position.

wale – the line formed between a vertical row of stitches.

wale deflection – distortion of the wales, usually caused by transferring stitches.

weaving – set the machine to weave or knitweave (see above).

welt – any ribbed or hemmed edge.

ACCESSORIES

There are many gadgets on the market for the machine knitter, but it is important to make sure that you will benefit from the extra devices before you buy them.

Blank Punchcards Cards without punched holes which enable you to punch your own cards to duplicate designs, or to create your own. Also available in rolls.

Bodkin The bodkin is a simple little tool. It looks just like an ordinary darning needle but has a hole at each end. You can use it for Swiss darning (page 130), binding off and transferring stitches just as you would with a transfer tool. I find it useful for transferring stitches from one bed to another.

Casting-on Comb For single bed machines this is a heavy metal bar with hooks, which is hung onto the stitches. For double bed machines it is a comb-like bar with eyelets which are threaded with wire to hold the stitches.

Charting Devices These are useful if you need to work the same shape in several gauges or a large repeat intarsia, lace or tuck pattern. You draw out your shape onto a sheet and do a gauge swatch. The gauge information is programmed into the machine and the sheet moves as you knit, telling you when to fashion or change color.

Color Changer Device which makes color changing automatic, up to four different colors can be selected at one time. On a double bed machine, a color changer enables you to knit rib jacquard or double bed jacquard or Fair Isle without floats.

Garter Bar A set of comb-like devices which transfer whole sections of stitches from one bed to another, or from the knit side to the purl side.

Garter Carriage This is an extra carriage which knits purl stitches on the right side of the work. It is quite a costly accessory for the home knitter and a bit slow.

Hand Punch Punch used with blank cards to make duplicate cards or produce original punchcards.

Intarsia Carriage This is a separate carriage which enables you to work intarsia fabrics. It is a useful accessory, now available for Passap machines.

Intarsia Yarn Brake This organizes your yarns so that they do not tangle while knitting intarsia. It takes 16 colors and extensions are available.

Lace Carriage An extra carriage which automatically selects needles from a punchcard and transfers the stitches to form lace fabrics. Usually used in conjunction with the main carriage, but some modern ones transfer and knit the stitch.

Multi-prong Transfer Tool This is a transfer tool with one point on one end and seven on the other. The seven can be locked in or out so that you can work with between one and seven points at one time. This tool is most useful for working wale deflection.

Needle Pusher Small ruler with a comb-like edge that is shaped in such a way that it will make a needle selection (often 1 × 1 or 2 × 2) so that needles can be quickly arranged for a rib, for example. Used for hand selection work and casting on. Some can be changed so that you are not confined to the needle arrangements offered by the manufacturer.

Ribbing Attachment A second bed of needles which fits onto the front of a single bed machine, enabling you to work professional ribs and interesting double bed structures and trims.

Stitch-related Graph Paper Graph paper that is printed with a grid of rectangles, rather than squares, to accommodate the shape of the stitch, which is wider than it is long. It prevents distortion of designs when they are knitted. It is also available as tracing paper, which makes it easier to transfer the design. See page 135.

Table Clamps These secure the machine to the table and keep it firmly in place. Also used for winders and twisters.

Transfer Lock Transfers stitches on double bed machines from one bed to the other. Some can transfer in complex patterns; others are more restricting.

Transfer Tool A tool used for transferring stitches, usually supplied with the machine. There are single, double and triple, i.e. tools with one, two or three prongs. Those with more prongs are used for cable work, wale deflection, etc. See multi-prong transfer tool above.

Waxer Wax block which is placed on the antenna. It automatically waxes the yarn as it passes through.

Weights Weights with little hooks hang onto the knitting or onto the cast-on comb (on double bed machines). They are used to take the work down.

Wool Winder A gadget which enables the knitter to wind neat balls of yarn from cones, hanks or skeins. Often it is best to take the yarn from the center of balls wound on winders.

Yarn Twister This enables you to twist together any combination of yarns to make your own yarn. There are several types available; some will only twist small amounts at one time. This involves you in endless winding so be careful to enquire exactly how they work when buying.

YARNS

The yarns used for the garments in the book are illustrated here at actual size. For best results, use the brands specified. If you are attempting to find a substitute, place a yarn of the same type next to the photograph to check that it is the same thickness.

T-shirt (page 66)
Rowan Soft Cotton (4-ply)

Denim Skirt (page 69)
Rowan Indigo Dyed Cotton 4-ply

Basic Shirt (page 72)
Rowan Soft Cotton (4-ply)

Ski Sweater (page 76)
Rowan Botany Wool (equivalent to 4-ply)

Slacks (page 80)
Rowan Botany Wool (equivalent to 4-ply)

Wrap (page 83)
Rowan Light Tweed (equivalent to 4-ply wool)
Rowan Botany Wool (equivalent to 4-ply)

Cream Suit (page 88)
Rowan Botany Wool (equivalent to 4-ply)

Dressy Sweater (page 92)
Todd & Duncan 100% 3-ply Cashmere

Cable Cardigan (page 95)
Rowan Botany Wool (equivalent to 4-ply)

Argyle Sweater (page 98)
Forsell 4-ply Wool
Rowan Botany Wool (equivalent to 4-ply)

Gansey Suit (page 102)
Forsell 4-ply Wool

Carpet Jacket (page 110)
Forsell 4-ply Wool
Rowan Botany Wool (equivalent to 4-ply)

Rowan Soft Cotton is a coned yarn. When sold in balls it is named Rowan Sea Breeze Soft Cotton.

Rowan Botany Wool, which is equivalent to a 4-ply wool yarn was used for all the stitch samplers and swatches and some of the garments. The colors given in the patterns are descriptive, and the code numbers of the yarns are given below:

cream = 1, pale yellow = 4, yellow = 6, mustard = 9, gold = 14, red = 26, slate = 54, mink = 102, black = 62, gray = 64, pale green = 89, green = 100, pastel green = 416, blue = 108, pale blue = 49, bright blue = 56, navy = 97, peach = 103, rust = 603, pink = 637.

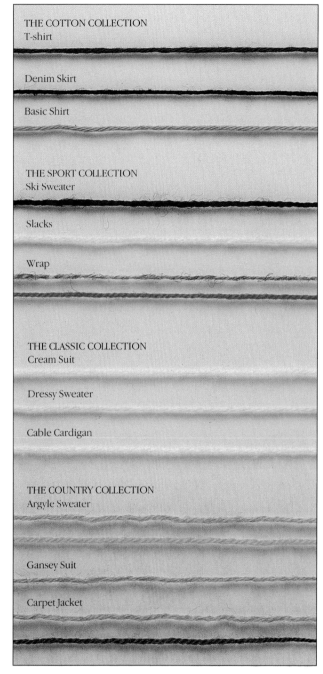

THE COTTON COLLECTION
T-shirt

Denim Skirt

Basic Shirt

THE SPORT COLLECTION
Ski Sweater

Slacks

Wrap

THE CLASSIC COLLECTION
Cream Suit

Dressy Sweater

Cable Cardigan

THE COUNTRY COLLECTION
Argyle Sweater

Gansey Suit

Carpet Jacket

SUPPLIERS

MACHINES

Brother International Corporation
8 Corporate Place,
Piscataway, N.J. 08855-0159
201-981-0300

KnitKing Corporation
1128 Crenshaw Blvd.
Los Angeles, CA 90019
213-938-2077

Passap Knitting Machines, Inc.
271 West, 2950 South
Salt Lake City, Utah 84115
801 485-2777

Singer Company
135 Raritan Center Parkway
Edison, N.J. 08837
201-632-6724

Studio Yarn Farms, Inc.
P.O. Box 46017
Seattle, WA 98146
206-763-1310

(Toyota) Newton's Knits, Inc.
3969 East La Palma
Anaheim, CA 92807
714-632-9861

White Sewing Machine Company
11750 Berea Road
Cleveland, Ohio 44111
216 252-3300

YARNS
In most cases throughout this book, I have used yarns supplied by Rowans. Many yarn manufacturers offer a mail order service and some will send you cards or lists of local suppliers on request.

Rowan Yarns
distributed by Westminster Trading Corp.
5 Northern Blvd.
Amherst, N.H. 03031

Anny Blatt
24770 Crestview Court
Farmington Hills, MI 48018

Berger du Nord
distributed by Bernat Yarn and Craft Corp.
Depot and Mendon Sts.
Uxbridge, MA 01569

Bramwell Yarns
P.O. Box 10729
Midland, Texas 79703

Brown Sheep
Route 1
Mitchell, NE 69357

Classic Elite Yarns, Inc.
12 Perkins St.
Lowell, MA 01854

Conshohocken Cotton Co.
550 Brook Rd.
Conshohocken, PA 19428

Crystal Palace Yarn
distributes Chanteleine yarn
3006 San Pablo Ave.
Berkeley, CA 94702

Delaine Worsted Mills
P.O. Box 951
Gastonia, NC 28055

Dyed in the Wool
distributes Patricia Roberts Yarn
252 West 37th St.
Suite 1800
New York, N.Y. 10018

Forsell and Emu
distributed by Plymouth Yarns
P.O. Box 28
Bristol, PA 19007

Joseph Galler, Inc.
27 West 20th St.
New York, N.Y. 10011

Gene Bailey Yarn Company
1238 Callow Hill Street
Suite 707
Philadelphia, PA 19123

Ironstone Warehouse
P.O. Box 196
Uxbridge, MA 01569

Knitting Machine Studio
72 East Palisade Avenue
Englewood, N.J. 07631

Lane Borgosesia
distributes Baruffa
RD 2 Fields Lane
North Salem, N.Y. 10560

Manos del Uruguay
Simpson/Southwick Co.
421 Hudson
New York, N.Y. 10014

Melrose Yarn Co.
1305 Utica Ave.
Brooklyn, N.Y. 11203

Merino Yarn Co.
distributes Georges Picaud yarn
320 West 37th St.
New York, N.Y. 10018

Phildar, Inc.
6110 Northbelt Parkway
Norcross, GA 30071

Pingouin
P.O. Box 100
Jamestown, S.C. 29453

Scott's Woolen Mill
P.O. Box 1204
Bristol, PA 19007

Silk City Fibers
155 Oxford St.
Patterson, N.J. 07522

Spring Brook Yarns
P.O. Box 122
Uxbridge, MA 01569

Tahki Yarns
11 Graphic Place
Moonachie, N.J. 07074

White Buffalo Mills, Inc.
123 3rd St.
P.O. Box 329
Pembina, ND 58271

ACCESSORIES

Hallandall, Inc.
P.O. Box 91
Rembrandt, IA 50576
Unicorn tool

Knit King Company
1128 Crenshaw Blvd.
Los Angeles, CA 90019
Yarn twister and intarsia carriage

Knittech
914 Warwickshire Ct.
Great Falls, VA 22066
Gauged graph paper

Knitting Machine Center
P.O. Box 15145
Cincinnati, OH 45215
Intarsia carriage for Passap

Kruh Knits
P.O. Box 1587
Avon Park North
Avon, CT 06001
Content and care labels
Double latch tool
Book holder

COMPARABLE NAMES OF MACHINES IN DIFFERENT COUNTRIES

Machines are sold under different brand names in different countries. Below is a list of the manufacturers and the names under which they sell their products in selected parts of the world.

Manufacturer	Brand Name	Country
Brother Corporation (Japan)	Brother	UK, Japan, USA, Canada Australia, NZ
	Knitking	USA
	Jones + Brother	UK and Eire
	Eva	Finland
Silver-Reed (Japan)	Knitmaster	UK and Eire
	Empisal	Europe (except UK), South Africa
	Studio	USA
	Singer	Canada, Australia, NZ, USA
	Silver	Japan
Aisin-Seiki (Japan)	Toyota	Worldwide
Madag (Switzerland)	Passap	UK, Europe, USA, Canada, Australia, NZ
	Pfaff	UK, Europe
Superba (France)	Singer	UK, Europe
	Phildar	Europe, USA
	Superba	Europe, Australia, South Africa
	White	USA, Canada

INDEX

ACKNOWLEDGMENTS

The publishers would like to thank the following for their help in the production of this book: Stephen Sheard and Kathleen Hargreaves at Rowan Yarns for supplying most of the yarn used in the book; Todd & Duncan for supplying the cashmere yarn; Barbara Jones (Artistic Licence) for hair and make-up; Linda Burns (Lynne Franks Ltd) for make-up; Annie (The Z Agency), Amelia Bryant and Lou Lou (Models One Elite), Eleanor Gordon and Liz Coppola (Bookings) and Jane Gee (Storm) for modeling the garments; Paul Smith, W. Yeoman (Chesterfield) Ltd Army Stores, and Bivouac of Matlock for clothes and accessories for the fashion photography.

Pattern Checkers
Mary Smith, Monica Bywaters, Hazel Ratcliffe

Fashion Photography
Ursula Steiger
Still-life Photography
Jacqui Hurst

Fashion Illustration
Sally-Anne Elliott
Step-by-step Illustration
Lindsay Blow
Charts
David Ashby

Typesetting
Bookworm Typesetting, Manchester
Reproduction
Evergreen, Hong Kong

Design
Louise Tucker

While every care has been taken to ensure that the knitting instructions in this book are accurate, Frances Lincoln Ltd cannot accept responsibility for any errors.

144